BENGAL VAISHNAVISM

BENGAL VAISHNAVISM

BIPIN CHANDRA PAL

With a Preface by Mr. Hirendra Nath Datta,
M. A., B. L., P. R. S., Vedanta-ratna.

GYAN

Published by

GYAN

Gyan Publishing House
5, Ansari Road
Daryaganj, New Delhi-110002
Phone: 011-47034999, 9811692060
E-mail: books@gyanbooks.com

Distribution Network
gyanbooks.com
India, USA, Canada, UK, Australia, France

ISBN: 978-81-212-8234-5 (PB)
First Published, 1933

2nd Impression 2023

Printed at: Gyan Press, Delhi.

BENGAL VAISHNAVISM
Author: BIPIN CHANDRA PAL

BENGAL VAISHNAVISM

BIPIN CHANDRA PAL

With a Preface by Mr. Hirendra Nath Datta,
M.A., B.L., P.R S., Vedanta-ratna.

CALCUTTA

MODERN BOOK AGENCY

10, College Square

1933

इहा आमि किछुइ ना जानि ।
ये तुमि कहाओ सेइ कहि आमि वाणी ॥
तोमार शिक्षाय पड़ि येन शुकपाठ ।
साक्षात् ईश्वर तुमि के बुझे तोमार नाट ॥

Naught, excepting this I know
That what from my lips doth flow
Is what thou bid'st me say.
And what I pour from out my throat
Parrot-like I learn by rote
From thee Lord !
A present God thou art, and none
Can fathom what by thee is done
In sport or playful mood.

(Rai Ramananda to Shree Chaitanya Mahaprabhu.)

PREFACE

In sending out into the world, what is practically the last contribution of my esteemed friend Mr. Bipin Chandra Pal to the Philosophy and Religion of Bengal Vaishnavism, not many words are needed by way of preface.

Mr. Bipin Chandra Pal was not only a political leader and an eloquent and convincing exponent of Indian Nationalism, but a profound student of the composite culture of his people. Though not a scholar in the technical and limited sense of the term, he was a deep student of the Indian religions and philosophies and a contemporary thought-leader in many ways. I knew him quite intimately. Dry-as-dust studies and collations of quotations would greatly bore him, but he had an instinctive and intuitional insight into Indian thought, both mediaeval and modern. His appreciation of Bengal Vaishnavism, with its unique contribution to Indian philosophical and religious thought, was truly profound and the reader who carefully studies the following pages will fully bear out this estimate.

Bengal, through the operation of forces—ethnic and historical—has developed a special culture of her own. No doubt, India is one cultural unit but inside the composite and far-flung civilization of India, the different provinces of the Indian continent have developed individual cultures (as Mr. Pal loved to expound in his own inimitable way), finding expression in their own cults, customs, languages and literatures.

The individuality of Bengali culture sought expression along two different lines—first, through the Shakti cult, where the Deity is conceived as the Universal Mother, and next, through the Krishna cult with its intoxicating love of the Lord and its spiritualisation of the ordinary human relations.

As expounded in Mr. Pal's "Bengal Vaishnavism", the Krishna cult of Bengal gave us a new philosophy, which departing from the Monism of Sankara and the Mono-dualisim of Ramanuja, made a notable departure in conceiving of the Deity as *Chidakara* and as the eternal embodiment of all the *Rasas.* This cult reached its efflorescence with Sri Chaitanya of Nadia, creating a new art and a new poetry —unique in its richness and romance—and profoundly affecting the moral and the social life of the Bengali people, with its protest against formalism and dogma and its simple faith and single surrender to the love of the Absolute.

Mr. Pal in the present volume has attempted, and I venture to think with considerable success, to re-interpret and re-explain the message of the Bengal Krishna-cult to the modern man, and I am sure that both in India and outside this country, his book will be read with profound interest and considerable profit by the people of different races and denominations, who happen to be interested in religion, philosophy, art and general culture.

HIRENDRA NATH DATTA.

October 16th, 1933.

CONTENTS

Bipin Chandra Pal

BENGAL VAISHNAVISM

CHAPTER I.

The Philosophy of the Absolute.

The notes and marks in the cultural and social life of Bengal, constituting the individuality of the Bengalee people, have found their highest organised expression in Bengal Vaishnavism. The literal meaning of Vaishnavism is the religion or cult of Vishnu, the second deity in the Hindu triad—Brahma the Creator, Vishnu the Preserver, and Shiva the Destroyer. The literal meaning of Vishnu is All-Pervasive. In this meaning the term is used in the Vedas, where it is said that the gods always see the Supreme Presence of Vishnu like extended objects in space. As the space is in itself invisible but we visualise it in seeing things that have dimension, so the all-pervasive Vishnu, though itself invisible, is recognised as the ground and subsistence of whatever material objects we are able to see with our eyes. As space is the logic of our knowledge of dimension, even so is this all-pervasive Vishnu the logic of all our visions of material objects. Vishnu has also been identified with the Sun-God. Many of our old Vaishnavic temples are therefore really temples for the sun. Vishnu is also identified with the Sky-God of the Vedas, the Jupiter of the Greeks. Though in the Hindu tradition Vishnu is the Preserver of the universe, in actual Vaishanvic thought he is practically conceived as Brahman, from Whom all objects have come to being, coming to being by Whom all objects continue to be, and towards Whom all objects move and into Whom all objects enter at the final dissolution. So Vishnu holds within Himself both Brahma the Creator and Shiva the Destroyer of the Hindu triad. The Vaishnavas worship Him not as a god but as the God. Vaishnavism, therefore, stands for what may be appropriately called Hindu theism.

But though Vaishnavism is found in all the Indian provinces as a Hindu school of thought and denomination of worshippers, both the philosophy and disciplines of Bengal Vaishnavism differ unmistakably from the

Vaishnavic cults of the other Indian provinces. Like other Hindu cults and cultures, Bengal Vaishnavism also accepts the Upanishads, the Brahma-Sutras and the Bhagavad-Geeta as its highest scriptural authority. But these universally-accepted scriptures have developed, through particular denominational interpretations, different theologies and spiritual cultures. The Bengal school of Vaishnavism has also developed its own philosophy through its interpretation of the Upanishads, the Brahma-Sutras and the Geeta. Samkara-Bhashya is the interpretation of the Brahma-Sutras of the Samkara-Vedanta school, the school of Absolute Monism. Shree-Bhashya of Ramanuja is the interpretation of the Vedanta of the Bhaktivada school of Southern India, the school of Qualified Monism. The Govinda-Bhashya of Baladeva Vidyabhusana is the canonical interpretation of the ancient Vedanta-Sutras or Brahma-Sutras acceptable to the school of Bengal Vaishnavas. But besides the Upanishads, the Brahma-Sutras and the Bhagavad-Geeta, Bengal Vaishnavas claim almost the same scriptural authority for the Shreemad-Bhagavata, which is designated by them as the fifth Veda.

The Bengal Vaishnava school accepts certain texts of these ancient scriptures as *Mahavakyas* or supreme revelations. All others must be interpreted by these fundamental texts. In the Upanishads the *Brahmananda Balli* of the Taittereeya Upanishad, which presents the Brahman as *Anandam*, is one of these *Mahavakyas.* In the Bhagavata Purana or Shreemad-Bhagavata the text describing the *Parama-Tattva* or the Ultimate Reality is another of these *Mahavakyas.* It is practically on these that the entire thought and realisations of the Bengal school of Vaishnavism have been built up by evidently a process of reasoning which is impossible to refute consistently with the actualities of our experience.

The Bhagavata text runs thus:

वदन्ति तत् तत्त्वविद स्तत्त्वं यज्ज्ञानमद्वयं
ब्रह्मेति परमात्मेति भगवानिति शब्द्यते ।

It means that those who know the *Tattva* or the Ultimate Reality, which answers all questions and removes all doubts, call that as *Tattva*, which is of the nature of Undivided Consciousness, called Brahman in the Upanishads, Paramatman or the Indweller by the followers of the way of *Yoga*, and Bhagavan by the adherents of the way of Love and

Faith or the *Bhakta.* Brahman, Paramatman and Bhagavan, these are three terms representing not three persons but the Absolute in three different aspects. Brahman represents the highest generalisation of cosmic experience and the final question regarding the origin, existence and dissolution of the universe. Brahman is the Unity that explains the infinite net of relations constituting this world of men and matter. Paramatman is the same Unity that explains the multiplicity and changes of our inner life, Who, as the Indweller, holds together the thread of our inner life and relations. But the cosmic life and the individual or personal life do not stand isolated but these are also bound up in a net of intimate relations. And the question is, who joins our personal consciousness to the outer objects in the universe and also to the similar personal consciousness of other individuals ? In short, who is the link between our senses and their objects in the cosmic creation, and who is the link that joins us to other human beings in bonds of love and service ? The answer to this question, according to Bengal Vaishnavism, is Bhagavan. Brahman is impersonal. Paramatman is the basis of our individual personality.

Bhagavan is the ground and explanation of our cosmic life and experience on the one side, and our social, including the domestic. life and experiences, on the other. Bhagavan is, therefore, not impersonal, but the Supreme Person, holding together our smaller and differentiated individual personalities. This, briefly, is the fundamental theological or philosophical position of Bengal Vaishnavism.

This Bhagavan is not an abstraction. Bhagavan is not a philosophical generalisation of human experience. Bhagavan is a concrete reality, a Person. The concept personality implies differentiation and duality. We realise ourselves as person through our relations first, with outer nature, where we are the knower and all natural objects, whether animate or inanimate, are objects of our knowledge. We are also moved by attractions and repulsions in our relations with these natural objects. And through these we realise ourselves as emotional beings. These objects are objects of our emotions. But here, that is, in simply knowing and feeling, our full personality is not realised. Knowing provokes feeling and feeling leads to action or desire for action.

Knowing, feeling and willing, therefore, complete the full content of our personality. And we realise it by a process of differentiation and integration. In the first stage, consciousness is quickened by a recognition of the differentiation between the knower and the known. But knowledge is completed, however, by the identification of the knower with the known either partially, when the object of knowledge is something particular, or wholly, when this object is something that covers and coincides with the totality of our whole being. This differentiation inside the unity of consciousness constitutes the essence of all our rational, emotional or volitional activities and experiences. In the theology of Bengal Vaishnavism, the Absolute is, therefore, neither entirely different from the cosmic or the human world, nor is the Absolute absolutely identified with these. Absolute duality leaves no room for relations, nor does absolute identity. Relation implies differentiation in unity. The theology of Bengal Vaishnavism is built upon this universal experience. It is not monistic like the Samkara-Vedanta school nor dualistic like Christianity, as popularly interpreted, or the Semitic theologies of Judaism and Islam, but really a synthesis of monism and dualism both. The Bengal Vaishnava school proclaims the relation between the Creator and His creation or the Brahman and the world, composed of both spirit and matter, as a relation of "inconceivable difference in identity and identity in difference", inconceivable because in formal logic identity and difference are two distinct categories. It cannot conceive that there may be difference inside identity and identity inside difference. The valid proposition in formal logic is, A is B or A is not B. But in transcendental logic we know that A may both be B and not-B.

The Absolute or the Ultimate Reality in Bengal Vaishnavism is both the Knower and the Object of His own knowledge. The Absolute is both the Enjoyer and the Object of His own enjoyment. The Absolute is the Agent or Worker and is Himself the Object upon which His will operates. In all these processes, whether of knowing or enjoying or working, the eternal motive is to ultimately cancel the differentiations with which knowing, enjoying and willing or acting start. At the beginning the knower stands apart from the object of his knowledge. In the end the knower is completely identified with his own object. This identification cancels all consciousness. But the Eternally Conscious Being cannot for a single moment exist in unconsciousness. Therefore, as soon as the unity of the subject and the object cancels consciousness, so soon again the subject separates himself from the object, and the movement of Reason starts again.

In Vaishnavic terminology unity or identity between the Absolute and the particular is called *pralaya* or dissolution, which means the cancellation of all relations. But immediately this identity is realised, differentiation starts again. This process of self-differentiation is called *sristi* or creation. It is an eternal process. In the language of philosophy it is the outward movement. It is culminated in the return of the self to itself, to use a Hegelian expression. This is *pralaya* in our terminology. *Sristi* or creation or differentiation ends in *pralaya* or integration and *sristi* re-starts immediately, ending in *pralaya* again. This process of differentiation and integration or *sristi* and *pralaya* is called *Leela* or the Sport of the Lord.

Leela or sport removes the suspicion of any necessity or compulsion. The Ultimate Reality creates this world, therefore, merely because He wills to do so. For the purposes of this creative sport, or what is called *Sristi Leela* in our Vaishnavic terminology, the Lord differentiates Himself from Himself and thus assumes a dual character. In one character, He is the Knower or the Subject. In another character, He is the Object of His own knowledge. Similarly, in one character He is the Enjoyer and the Agent or Actor, while in another character, He is the Object of His enjoyment and of His will or action The Knower, the Enjoyer and the Agent or the Actor is called the *Purusha*, while the Object of the Lord's knowing, enjoying and willing is called *Prakriti*. *Prakriti* and *Purusha* are, however, not two beings but the one and the same being, self-differentiated for the creative process or the creative sport of the Lord.

The whole structure of the philosophy and art of Bengal Vaishnavism is built upon the conception of the *Purusha* and *Prakriti*. The terms are not peculiar to Vaishnavic thought. They are the central terms of the Sankhya system. But in the Sankhya system *Purusha* and *Prakriti*, though co-related in creation,—

and as creation is not something that takes place in time, both the *Purusha* and the *Prakriti* are eternal entities, co-eternal and co-existent with one another,—yet they are not one and the same being. In the Samkara-Vedanta monism *Purusha* and *Prakriti* are not real and eternal elements of the Divine Consciousness, Which knows no differentiation or duality, Wherein there is neither knowing nor feeling, as we know these in our own experience. In absolute monism, who sees, with what, and whom? Who knows, whom, with what? Brahman is Pure Consciousness, and Pure *Anandam* and Pure Existence. If still the Samkara-Vedanta school uses the terms *Purusha* and *Prakriti*, they do not represent Reality but are only conceived through *Maya* or Illusion, incidental to the creative process. What we call Personal God, the Iswara of the Samkara-Vedanta, is, therefore, not the Absolute in its truth and essence, but is only a moment or phase of our experience of the Absolute at a certain stage of our own consciousness. When all duality has been cancelled, as it is and must be in the highest state of illumination, when all personal or individual consciousness is absolutely merged in the Universal Consciousness or Brahman, then Iswara himself is also merged in Brahman, and there remains no Personal God.

In Bengal Vaishnavism, which is also essentially monistic, though its monism is not the same as the monism of the Samkara-Vedanta school, ***Purusha*** and ***Prakriti*** are one and the same, but they are differentiated in the creative process for purposes of ***Leela***. This self-differentiation is an assumption as by different characters in a stage play. In this sense the personality of God comes very near the conception of personality in Christianity itself. ***Persona*** means a mask in Latin, and the Divine Personality is, therefore, something which is assumed, or a mask put on, by the Absolute for the same objects as in Vaishnavism, namely, the self-differentiation of the Absolute for the realisation of consciousness or self-realisation.

Differentiation necessarily implies integration. The Sport or ***Leela*** of the Lord, which is the very plinth and foundation of the philosophy and art of Bengal Vaishnavism, is, therefore, an eternal process of differentiation and integration, the ***Prakriti*** separating Herself from the ***Purusha*** and eternally striving to be re-united to Him. This is the central idea in the whole scheme of Bengal Vaishnavism. Bengal Vaishnavism has always repudiated the Samkara-Vedantic doctrine of *Maya* or Illusion as rank heresy. To it the world is real. All social relations are real. Nature and man are both real. But this reality has two aspects; one, what may be called the eternally realised aspect; the other, the progressively realising aspect. The world, as we see it, is in a process of progressive realisation. But the explanation of this progressive realisation must be sought and found in that aspect of the world wherein it is eternally realised. All objects, natural and human, and all relations in this world exist in their eternally realised state in the Being of the Lord. The sun, the moon, the starry heaven, the vegetable world, the animal and the human world,—all these exist in their eternally realised perfection in the Being of the Lord. All these are elements of His *Prakriti.* This *Prakriti* exists from eternity to eternity in the Being of the Lord, though for purposes of *Leela* differentiated from Him from eternity to eternity. In creation, or more correctly speaking, in the creative process, all objects, natural and human, exist as progressively realising themselves, moving from the less perfect to the more perfect. This world has, therefore, its true meaning and purpose not here but in the very Being of the Lord. The world is not *mayik* or illusory. It is not a dream or a nightmare. But it is real, eternally real, in the Being of the Lord. All the relations of the world are real, though progressively realising here, real in their prototype, in the Being of the Lord, as eternally realised relations. All our emotions have their root and realisation in the Being of the Lord; and while in a state of progressive realisation here below they exist as eternally realised there in the very Being of the Lord. The Lord or the Ultimate Reality is not an abstraction as He practically is in the Samkara-Vedanta thought, but what may be called the Concrete Universal. There in His own eternally realised Being the Lord is Himself the Knower or Subject and that which He knows or the Object, the Enjoyer and that through which He realises His enjoyment, the Actor or Worker and that upon which He works His will. In His eternally realised Being He is Himself the Lord or Master and Himself His own Valet or Servitor, Himself the Father and He is Himself His own Son, He is Himself Friend and the object of His friendship, He is Himself the Lover and the object of His love. When we call God Father, if our realisation of fatherhood be real and not merely a poetic or devotional fancy, then we must conceive in His own Being a Son, eternally realised like Himself as the absolute condition of His own Fatherhood. This has been seized by Christianity. But this only. The multiplicity of our human relations of love and affection and service have not been tried to be realised in God by the ordinary Christian conception or consciousness. This has been done by Bengal Vaishnavism. God is not only our Father, He is our Master, our Friend, our Children and our Lover. All these relations of love and service here below, if they are true and real, must have their eternally realised prototype organised in the very Being of the Lord. This is what Bengal Vaishnavism has tried to do. The Ultimate Reality does not exist in Himself as in-differentiated Unity or Consciousness but as self-differentiated congeries of relations there in His own Being. He is in a link or net of spiritual relations between Himself and His *Prakriti* as eternally realised or eternally perfect Father, responding eternally to the loving loyalty of the eternally perfect Son, or more correctly, Sons. Similarly, all the other relations of our own life here below exist eternally realised in Him through His *Prakriti* As we are domestic and social beings here, realising ourselves in an organised society, so stands the Lord in an organised spiritual society of His own, composed of the endless multiplied forms of His *Prakriti*. And the exquisite romance of love and service which we taste here in our earthly life has its prototype in the love-play in His own Being. The bogey of anthropomorphism that has scared away the thought and theology of the other world-religions from this inexorable logic of thought, did not influence Bengal Vaishnavic thought, which was not afraid of carrying the logic of man's direct personal experience and realisations into the very Being of the Lord without which these experiences and relations could not possibly be justified rationally and spiritually, and had therefore to be dismissed either as illusions or snares of the Satan. Bengal Vaishnavism refused to do either. And it, therefore, posited the root and realisatiou of all our human relations and affections in the eternally realised personality of God. The Vaishnavic conception of heaven, which is called

Brindabana, is the logic of the evolution of this world of Nature, man and society. In Brindabana all Nature stands in its perfected beauty. In Brindabana humanity stands in all the perfections of its life and relations, the perfections towards which individual human and social groups have been striving from eternity to eternity. In Brindabana the law is not the law of force, direct or indirect, physical, mental or social; but the supreme law of pure and self-less love. In Brindabana, lastly, there are no gods or supernatural beings but only perfected humans, perfect in body, in mind, in emotions and in will. The heaven, as conceived by Bengal Vaishnavism, is nothing more or less than what is called for by the inexorable logic of our earthly existences and experiences. Shree Chaitanya Mahapravu in his historic discussion with the learned expositor of Samkara-Vedantism, Swami Prakasananda in Benares summed up the philosophy of the Absolute of his school with these words:

ब्रह्मशब्दे मुख्य अर्थे कहे भगवान
चिदैश्वर्य्य परिपूर्ण अनूर्द्ध समान ।
तांहार विभूतिदेह सब चिदाकार
चिद्विभूति आच्छादिया कहे निराकार ॥

"The term Brahman, in its essential meaning, refers to Bhagavan, Who is filled with spiritual attributes and power. None is equal to or higher than He. His manifestations and body are all spiritual. Ignoring these spiritual characters (the Samkara-Vedanta) calls Him as without body or differentiations."

This is the central position of the Bengal school of Vaishnavism in regard to the nature and attributes of the Divine Being. God has no form, say both Christianity and Islam. He is formless or *nirakara* says the Hindu of the Vedantic school. Even popular Hinduism, which makes numerous forms of the Deity for purposes of its worship, does not accept these forms as real and true. They are fanciful creations of the devotees, created for purposes of worship with a view to render the contemplation and love of God easy to the unillumined crowd, who cannot conceive of a formless God, much less cultivate sentiments of devotion to Him in the present stage of their existence as embodied spirits. Formlessness means to the multitude really a void, absolute emptiness. We cannot worship or cultivate personal devotion towards a void. Yet our mind and heart yearn after our Maker. The

Hindu Vedanteen says that man cannot in his natural state know or love God. The contemplation of Brahman in truth and reality is possible only in that state of absolute *yogic* concentration called *samadhi*; wherein the eye sees not its objects, the ear hears not any sound, the other senses cease absolutely to sense their objects, the mind thinks not and all contact and connection between our consciousness and this outer world of sights and sounds are completely cut off. This state of *samadhi* is really a state of negation. In fact, it is neither a state of consciousness nor unconsciousness. It is the state of what may be called pure being, which is equal to pure nothing in Hegelian thought. This pure being is undifferentiated consciousness, wherein all relations are cancelled, and therefore all knowing and thinking, as we understand these terms, also cease. Bengal Vaishnavic thought also believes in that state of supreme concentration, wherein the outer sense-contacts cease as in *samadhi*, but this *samadhi* is not empty *samadhi* but it comes from the losing of our senses, our thought and our understanding and all our emotions in the realisation of the Lord. The familiar expression of this Vaishnavic *samadhi* is:

स्थावर जङ्गम देखे देखे ना तार मूर्त्ति
यांहा नेत्र पड़े हय इष्टदेवस्फूर्त्ति ।

which means the devotee sees with his eyes all objects, both those that move not and those that move, but he sees not their outer form; wherever his eyes fall there is revealed the form of the Object of his devotion. In other words, in the state of *samadhi* the devotee is lost completely in the consciousness of his Lord. This is a verified and verifiable experience. To the Christian devotee in this state of *samadhi* it is the Christ who fills and covers all things. To the Moslem devotee it is Mahomet who fills and covers all objects. The Christian or the Moslem devotee sees even with his outer eyes not material objects or forms upon which his vision falls, but the form of Christ or Mahomet. This is a not very uncommon experience even in our human relations of love-romance. The lover losing all outer consciousness becomes possessed by the form and the voice and even the odour of the object of his or her love, though objectively he or she may not be present before the senses. In the records of the experiences of Christian devotees it is not unknown. St. Francis of Assissi, we learn, found thus the passion of

Christ reproduced in his own person, and he was so identified not only with the mind and will of his Master, but even with his physical experiences upon the Cross that blood rushed out of his hands, feet and temple at the points which were nailed to the Cross in the body of Christ himself. This is practically the same as the supreme beatitude of our Vaishnavic saints and devotees.

In Bengal Vaishnavic culture the Ultimate Reality is called Shree Krishna. Shree Krishna is the *Purusha* or the Supreme Person of our Vaishnavic thought. And Shree Radha is the name for His *Prakriti.* Radha Krishna are, however, really not two but One. It is in the process of the self-realisation of the Divine Unity that the Supreme Person becomes differentiated into *Purusha* and *Prakriti.* Shree Krishna and Shree Radha are essentially one. But this unity of the Divine Being is not an undifferentiated unity, but is eternally self-differentiated. In this self-differentiation Shree Krishna stands as the *Purusha* and Shree Radha His *Prakriti*, that by and through which He realises His consciousness or His rational being, His love or His emotional being, and His will or volitional being. Shree Krishna is the eternal Subject. Shree

Radha is the eternal Object by and through which Shree Krishna realises His consciousness or rational being. Shree Krishna is similarly the eternal Enjoyer, and Shree Radha is the eternal Object in and through whom Shree Krishna realises His emotional being. Similarly, Shree Krishna is Eternal Will, and Shree Radha is the eternal Object upon whom Shree Krishna works His will and thus realises his volitional being. This, briefly, is the realisation of Bengal Vaishnavism of the nature of the Ultimate Reality.

This Ultimate Reality or Shree Krishna is not without form or *nirakara*, but as Shree Chaitanya declared, *chidakara*. *Chidakara* is distinguished, on the one side, from material or sensusus form and, on the other side, from *nirakara* or no form. There is a great deal of confusion in most minds regarding this concept form or *akara* in Sanskrit. Most people think that *akara* or form must be material and sensuous, and as they cannot, very correctly no doubt, conceive of the Ultimate Reality as having a material form, they rush to the conclusion that the Supreme Being must necessarily be *nirakara* or without any form whatever. This is what our own Samkara-Vedantic thought has done. This is also what popular Christianity as well as the Semitic systems, Judaism and Islam, have done. In all these systems God is conceived as without form. But these conceptions are clearly due to a confused understanding of what 'form' really means and implies. The central idea of form is that which separates one object from another. In our ordinary sense-experience the dividing line between one thing and another is material. Therefore, we naturally rush to the conclusion that form must necessarily be something material, cognisable by our eyes or the other senses. But that this is not the essential connotation of the term form is even admitted by the crowd who speak of thought-form. Thought-forms, organised in words, in literature, are not admittedly material forms. The real concept of form, therefore, is something that separates or differentiates one object from another. And the question is, must this 'something' necessarily be something material or realised by outer senses? The logic of all worship leads irresistibly to the existence of 'form' as the essential element of differentiation between the worshipper and the Object of his worship; and that by which the worshipper realises himself as the worshipper and his Deity as the object of his worship is really the 'form' of his God.

This is as much true of the popular image worship of the Hindu as of those who claim to worship their God in "truth and in spirit". Only the Samkara-Vedanteen, who holds that he and his Brahman are absolutely one, and worship consists in the realisation of this absolute unity between him and the Object of his worship, wherein there is absolutely no consciousness of duality or differentiation, need not admit even realisation of non-material form as an essential condition of Divine worship. In fact, in true realisation even the consciousness of the worshipper and the worshipped must also cease. The formula of Vedantic realisation is: "I am He or Brahman." The complete realisation of this truth is what the Vedanteen understands by *moksha* or salvation. The Samkara-Vedanta here emphasises only one point in the Being of the Absolute, wherein the process of consciousness ends after differentiation into integration. The Bengal Vaishnava thought conceives the Absolute as the entire process of consciousness. The process has been clearly indicated by the Hegalian dictum: The self separates itself from itself to return to itself to be itself. This process cannot be broken up at any particular point. Nor can there be any consciousness except in and through this process. Therefore, when integration is reached, consciousness also necessarily ceases. But the Absolute is eternally self-conscious. Absolute Consciousness can never cease. This is the Vaishnavic position. Integration, therefore, means, as has been already said, *pralaya*. The Samkara-Vendanta takes a static view of the Absolute, and, therefore, conceives this integration or *pralaya* as the real state of the Absolute. The Vaishnava-Vedanta of Bengal conceives the Absolute not merely in its static aspect but also equally in its dynamic aspect. Differentiation and integration are not complete in themselves. They are both links in the chain of consciousness. Differentiation and integration are both essential elements or moments of the Absolute Consciousness or Brahman. As in the reality of the Absolute there is this eternal differentiation and integration, so also in Divine worship there is always this consciousness of difference between the worshipper and the worshipped. The Bengal Vaishnava does not aim at complete merging of the worshipper with the Object of his worship. He, therefore, says that even if he is offered this complete merging with the Lord, he does not accept it; because his aim and object is not to be Brahman but to eternally love and worship Brahman. The familiar dictum of Ramakrishna Paramahansa: "I do not want to be sugar, I want to taste it," clearly explains this Vaishnavic position. Worship of the Lord is necessary according to the Samkara-Vedanta thought only in a lower stage of spiritual evolution. In the highest stage of illumination, when all individual consciousness is completely merged in the Universal Consciousness, there is no worship, and, therefore, the consciousness of form, though it be not material but spiritual form, is not necessarily implied in Vedantic monism. But in every other system, whether Hindu Vaishnavic or Shaiva or Christian or Islam or Judaic, which accepts the worship of the Lord as an eternal duty, we must concede to the Lord some notes or marks of differentiation from His worshipper. Bengal Vaishnavism declares that these notes or marks or, in a word, this 'form' of the Lord is not material but spiritual. The Lord, therefore, is not without form but has a spiritual form of His own. The Lord is not without body but has a spiritual body. He is not without senses or sense-organs but has spiritual senses or sense-organs.

Then again, those who believe in life after death or the continuity of the human personality after the dissolution of the physical organism in and through which this personality expresses and realises itself on the plane of the living, must posit some form or note or mark or differentiation by which these personalities can be recognised on the other side, which recognition is a fundamental postulate of our faith in life after death. All these similarly irresistibly drive us to the conclusion that the human spirit or soul and the Divine or the Universal Spirit or God, both must have spiritual forms by means of which they stand differentiated from one another and through which can only one spirit recognise another spirit in the spirit-world. Shree Chaitanya's philosophy of the Absolute, as summed up very briefly in his reply to the Samkara-Vedantic doctrine of absolute monism, is evidently derived from these examinations and analyses of universal psychological experiences.

An analysis of our sense-experiences in the light of the law of evolution also lends support to Shree Chaitanya's philosophy of the Absolute. The Absolute or *Paramatattva*, which may be translated into English as the Ultimate Reality, in Bengal Vaishnavism is not without form or body, but has a spiritual body of its own. This physical body, which evolves from what is called a primary cell in biology, must have for its Regulative Idea a perfect and eternally realised form of the body into which it ultimately develops. This 'form' is not a thing of flesh and blood. Flesh and blood merely organise the *idea*. Behind our physical body this *idea* can only be what is called a spiritual idea. Our physical bodies posit, therefore, at the back of their biological evolution an eternally realised *idea* or spiritual form. In comparing the beauty of different human bodies we refer them to a universal human form, universal or infinite not as covering all space but as an embodiment of the highest perfection of the body. It is in the light of this eternally realised and absolutely perfect human body or form that we make these comparisons of good, better and best, and are able to pass our aesthetic judgment on them. This perfected human form is the logic of all our conceptions of and judgment on the beauty of the human body. In the realisations of Bengal Vaishnavism this eternally realised and eternally perfect human body is the spiritual form or body of the Lord. It differs from our physical body in this, namely, that while our physical body is subject to growth, disease and decay, that are characteristic of all flesh, the Body of the Absolute or Shree Krishna is not and cannot be subject to the common ailments of our flesh. It knows no growth, it knows no decay, is not subject to dissolution. It is eternally realised, eternally perfect, and as such stands as the Regulative Idea of our own frames of flesh. This is really what the realisations of Bengal Vaishnavism mean when these speak of the essentially human form of Shree Krishna.

The same remark equally applies to our physical senses and the organs of our sense-knowledge. The eye, the ear, all these pass through processes of evolution. These organs develop gradually in the womb of our mother. This process irresistibly posits eternally realised and perfect forms of these different sense-organs. These are not and cannot possibly be carnal or composed of flesh and blood, though they are organised through flesh and blood during the process of their evolution in the human body. The primary cell from which this body has developed had no sense-organs. They existed and could possibly exist only as what we call an *idea*. All evolution is really the evolution of an *idea*. This *idea* is, however, not a figment of our fancy, but an eternally realised spiritual entity. This is what Shree Chaitanya referred to as *Chidaisvarya*. All these psychological experiences, therefore, irresistibly force the conclusion that Brahman or the Absolute from Whom this world has come into being, Who is the origin of both what we call Nature and Man, is not and cannot possibly be formless or *nirakara*; nor can He possibly have a carnal body and carnal senses like those with which we are endowed, but must have an eternally realised and eternally perfect spiritual body of His own, organised in and through spiritual organs of perception and emotion and will, through which He holds together in His own Consciousness this universe of sense-objects and by means of which He eternally enjoys these objects and works His own will upon them.

As Shree Chaitanya pointed out, the central concept of the Absolute in the Bengal Vaishnava school is Bhagavan. The term is, no doubt, in common use both among the followers of the Samkara-Vedanta and the followers of Shree Chaitanya. But the latter have carried the logic of this concept Bhagavan to its utmost reality. Bhagavan means literally one who is possessed of what are called *bhaga*-s in Sanskrit. These *bhaga*-s are, (i) *Aisvarya**—sense-objects,—"*shabda*, *sparsa*, *rupa*, *rasa*, *gandha*" or sound, touch, vision, taste and smell—objects that have these qualities; (ii) *Veerya*, which means the potency or strength of the senses of sight, audition, touch etc.; (iii) *Yasha* or good repute; (iv) *Shree* or that which attracts others to oneself; (v) *Jnanam*—knowledge or illumination; (vi) *Vairagya* or freedom from attachment and repulsion. Bhagavan means one who has in him these six *bhaga*-s in their entirety. In plain language Bhagavan is He Who holds within Himself all sense-objects in their essence, Who has the full capacity of the senses to hold and enjoy all sense-objects, Who possesses all good repute, Who has in its fullest measure the quality of attracting (other beings), Who has

---

* *Aisvarya* literally means possessions and powers. It also means psychic or occult or spiritual or *yogic* powers. It is in this sense that the term is popularly interpreted by mediaeval Hindu thought. But as in the definition of Bhagavan this *Aisvarya* is related to *Veerya*, which means the power of the senses to seize and enjoy their objects, *Aisvarya* here must mean sense-objects.

all knowledge, and complete aloofness from both attachment and repulsion. This Bhagavan holds within Himself all sense-objects. In other words, the whole universe of both matter and men exist in the very Being of Bhagavan. He is not without sense-organs, though his sense-organs are not like our sense-organs physical, but spiritual.

The senses exist organised in our bodies; Bhagavan has also His body, though it is not like our bodies made of mortal flesh. Bhagavan has also a social organism, the contents of which are spirit like Himself, of the same kind or class as Himself but differing from Him in that they are not independent existences but dependent on Him for their existence and activities. Bhagavan not only has the power of attraction in Him but as no power exists in the abstract, He has in His own being those whom He constantly attracts by His own qualities. This is the logic of the term Bhagavan as applied to the Absolute. And these are the contents of the conception of the Absolute or what may be called the Concrete Universal in the Vaishnavic thought of Bengal.

In our Vaishnavic thought and realisation the world, therefore, is not unreal or an illusion. It is not even what is popularly called relatively real, but absolutely real, though here in our experience this reality is a progressively realising reality, which exists eternally realised in the Being of Bhagavan. In this, Bengal Vaishnavism (and generally more or less all the Vaishnavic schools of Hinduism) stands differentiated from the popular mediaeval thoughts and philosophies of India that are fatally obsessed by the Vedantic dogma of *Maya* or Illusion ; and wherein the negation of this world, as distinguished from its spiritualisation or idealisation, is an overwhelming note, with the result that renunciation of the world, supression of all natural instincts, however healthy, and the repudiation of all normal obligations of human love and affection became a dominant note in the religious life ond spiritual endeavours of this medieval Hinduism. Bengal Vaishnavism entered a strong protest against these. It frankly accepted the fundamental truths of mediaeval Vedantic culture and therefore did not absolutely repudiate the fundamental disciplines of so-called asceticism and monasticism, but only corrected its false philosophy and abnormal excesses. The object of asceticism is not the supression of the natural desires and appetites of the flesh, but their regulation. This regulation is absolutely essential, in fact, for even the very enjoyment of these appetites and desires. But even this regulation, though it must form the very plinth and foundation of the spiritual life, must fail of its purpose unless it has as its objective, spiritualisation or idealisation. Bengal Vaishnavism pursues this process of idealisation and spiritualisation of all our sense-activities, culminating in the realisation of the *Anandam* of the Lord Himself in and through our relations of love and service. For this idealisation it is essential that the devotee should establish his complete mastery over his senses and free himself from the domination of sense-contacts and the sense-life over his inner spiritual life. This is an essential pre-condition of the pursuit of the way of *Bhakti* or Love of God, which is the objective of our Vaishnavic culture. It repudiates absolute asceticism, which really is not detachment or *vairagya* but is found at the ultimate analysis to be even a worse form of attachment itself, which results from a consciousness of conflict and not the realisation of that higher synthesis wherein there is neither good nor evil but both are subsumed as spokes in the wheel of the Ultimate All-Good. It accepts, however, the essential point in asceticism, which is meant to secure the freedom of the spirit from the domination of the flesh. Vaishnavic discipline seeks to secure this freedom by consecrating all our senses and our domestic and social relations to the Lord. When the conceit of our personality or individuality is completely cured, and with the elimination of all self-regarding desires in the pursuit of our sense-life and the pleasures and obligations of the domestic and social relations, these are completely transfigured as the *leela* or the sport of the Lord Himself, the Vaishnavic ideal is realised, so far as such realisation of the Absolute is possible within the limitations of man's earthly life.

To sum up, the Absolute or the Ultimate Reality in Bengal Vaishnavic thought is not *nirakara* or formless—a mere abstraction or generalisation of our experiences but is a Concrete Reality. As a Person He stands differentiated from all other objects and persons in creation. Therefore, He has necessary notes and marks constituting the elements of this differentiation. These notes and marks are fundamental and necessary elements of what we understand by form or body. The Absolute, therefore, has a body, but not a mortal body like ours, which is subject to growth and decay. But even this body cannot be explained unless it has as its Regulative Idea an eternally realised ideal or prototype. That prototype cannot be something physical or material but must necessarily be non-physical and non-material or what we understand as spiritual. The Absolute has a non-material, non-physical or spiritual body. Only to seize this truth we must first of all completely get rid of the very common conception of the Infinite as a Spacial Infinite. All our confusions regarding the Absolute or most of these arise from this wrong notion. The Absolute has also sense-organs similar to ours, though unlike our organs His organs are not physical and material. Indeed, even our sense-organs are really not absolutely physical or material. Behind these organs, clothed in flesh, there stand spiritual essences, wherein we have to seek and find their truth and meaning. Our sense-organs are subject to the universal law of evolution ; they grow from less to more ; they are subject to growth and decay. But this process of evolution cannot be rationally understood or explained unless on the assumption that there stand behind these organs eternally realised organs which constitute the Regulative Idea in the evolution of our sense-organs. The Absolute has eternally realised organs of His own. He has the organ of sight. This visible universe is held together in and by His vision or the visual organ. Similarly, He has an eternally realised organ of audition, wherein is held together the entire universe of sound. And so on and so forth. And as these organs are not merely organs of knowledge but as every contact of these organs with their objects produces joy or *Anandam*, the Absolute in the conception of Bengal Vaishnavism is not only not without body, but His body is the organisation of all joy, all romance, all love and all happiness. He is called *Nikhila-rasamritamurti* or the embodiment of eternal joy and eternal bliss.

But the boldest and the grandest achievement of the Vaishnava thought of Bengal is its conception of the Absolute as the Perfected Man. This idea is older than Shree Chaitanya Mahapravu, the founder of the Bengal school of Vaishnavism. It was, therefore, really the realisation or revelation of the age-long genius and culture of the Bengalee people, which proves that there must have been what may be called a Humanistic school of Bengalee thought and theology before Shree Chaitanya, from which his own Vaishnavism must have received its inspiration. The Bengalee poet Chandidasa, who was born quite a hundred years before Shree Chaitanya, delivered the message of this Humanism in the remarkable verse :

शुन हे मानुष भाइ !
सबार उपरे मानुष सत्य
ताहार उपरे नाइ ।

which means, "Hear O Brother Man ! Above all is the Truth of Man ; there is none higher than this." The divinity of man as *guru* had been proclaimed by the Bengal school of Buddhism. Upto this day many Hindu sects in Bengal worship their *guru* as their God. This doctrine of the *guru* has been an attempt to universalise the doctrine of historical incarnation. The need which led to the doctrine of incarnation failed to be completely met by it. The Absolute is unknown and unapproachable. He has, for purposes of our realisation, to come down to our plane, to be revealed in the flesh, assume a human form and character. But this incarnation did not or could not continue on this plane eternally. When, therefore, a Christ or a Buddha passed away, the need of humanity for an ever-present Human Deity still remained. This necessity was sought to be met by the dogma of Popery in Christendom, and by the dogma of the *guru* in Buddhism and Hinduism. The *guru* is an individual man, endowed with divine powers. Chandidasa, however, went further than the apotheosis of the *guru*, which had already been familiar to both Hinduism and Buddhism. He delivered his message to all men—"Hear O Brother Man !" In this he proclaimed also the doctrine of what is called the Brotherhood of Man, which is a necessary corollary to the doctrine of the Divinity of Man. Bengal Vaishnavism developed this declaration of Chandidasa in its philosophy and art. In the theology of Bengal Vaishnavism the Ultimate Reality or *Paramatattva* is Bhagavan. This Bhagavan is Shree Krishna. **कृष्णस्तु भगवान स्वयम्।** Shree Krishna is Bhagavan Himself. The significance of the word **स्वयम्** or himself in this text is that this Shree Krishna, who is realised by Bengal Vaishnavism as Bhagavan or the Ultimate Reality is not an incarnation.

While every school of the Krishna cult in Hinduism regards Shree Krishna as an incarnation of the Lord, it is the Bengal school only which rejects this dogma as heresy, and declares that Shree Krishna, who is the object of Vaishnavic worship in Bengal, is not an incarnation of the Lord but the very Lord Himself. The Chaitanya Charitamrita, which is regarded as the special scripture of the Bengal school of Vaishnavism, says that Shree Krishna is "*avataree*" or That from which all *avatara*-s or incarnations proceed or emanate. He is Himself not an incarnation or emanation, but the root and origin of all incarnations and emanations. In the Bhagavata Purana, however, Shree Krishna has been counted as an *avatara* by Shukdeva. But Shukdeva repented of this sin against the Lord, and, therefore, he corrected himself subsequently by declaring that Shree Krishna was not an incarnation or emanation of the Lord but the Lord Himself. And this Shree Krishna of Bengal Vaishnavism is different from the Shree Krishna of the clan of the Yadus, the Shree Krishna of the Mahabharata epic. The Shree Krishna whom the Bengal Vaishnavas worship never moves from Brindabana. Brindabana, as we have seen, is the eternally realised prototype of the progressively realising universe in the midst of which we live. This Brindabana is in the very Being of the Lord. And when Shree Krishna never moves from His Eternal Being or State, He cannot be an incarnation or emanation; because, such incarnation or emanation is inconceivable unless He moves from His eternal state. This is the logic of the Bengal Vaishnavic position in regard to Shree Krishna. This Shree Krishna is always of the human form—two-handed, never four-handed or six-handed, as he has been described in the popular Krishna cult and legend. These four-handed or six-handed conceptions are imaginary and fanciful made by the devotees to help them in their devotions. They are not the real form of Shree Krishna. All these have been expressly declared in the scriptures of Bengal Vaishnavism. Summing up these conceptions of the Divine Personality the Bengal Vaishnavas declare:

कृष्णेर यतेक लीला सर्व्वोत्तम नरलीला
नरवपु ताहार सहाय ।

Of all the sports of Shree Krishna the highest and best is that acted on the human plane; in this sport His instrument or help is the human body.

In this conception of Shree Krishna as the Lord or Bhagavan, Bengal Vaishnavic thought has followed the inexorable logic of the general Vedantic position as distinguished from the position of the Samkara-Vedantic school. Brahman is both the efficient and the material cause of the universe. This is the general Vedantic position. Following the logic of it, Vedantic thought tried to explain this universe by positing Brahman behind it. What Bengal Vaishnavism did, however, was to go further and ask itself, if the explanation of the universe is that it has emanated from Brahman, the question arises, is this emanation *real* or only apparent ? Popular Vedantism, and in this term must be included ordinary Vaishnavism also, declares that it is not real but only apparent. Bengal Vaishnavism, however, as I have already indicated, believes in the reality of the universe, not outside but in the very Being of the Lord. It is from there, where this universe exists eternally realised, that it has emanated, and been manifested as a progressively realising reality. Not only this universe but man also exists in the very Being of the Lord eternally realised. And of this spiritual human kingdom, composed of eternally realised humans, Shree Krishna stands as the centre. He is the Lord and Master of this eternally realised human kingdom. But here He rules only and absolutely through love, and not through fear or awe. The soul of love is the sense of kinship, instinct with the spirit of equality. In sport, all the players, though playing different parts, are not dominated by any sense of inferiority or fear. What we call democracy really reigns in the play-ground. The subordination of the different players to their leader or captain is really self-determined and not superimposed from above or outside, and therefore breeds no conceit of superiority or sense of inferiority. This is the conception of Brindabana as a social ideal in Bengal Vaishnavism. Shree Krishna is made to almost lament the universal usage of His worshippers, who stand in fear of Him, in awe of His might and majesty. And He desires for the pure love and affection of His devotees, unmoved by any consciousness of His greatness and grandeur. He wants, He says, the simple love of His devotees. "The mother-love that chastises me, the friend who challenges my superiority and rides on my back and offers me his food out of his own mouth, the lover who in a fit of anger charges me with infidelity and sends me away from her,—all these are infinitely more pleasing to me than the hymns of the Vedas that proclaim my glory." All these present an exquisite democratic ideal of *Bhakti* or Love of God. In this Bengal Vaishnavism has organised in theology and devotion the age-long genius and individuality of the Bengalee people.

CHAPTER II.

The Bengal Bhakti Cult.

The *Bhakti* cult in Bengal is one of the distinct features of the genius and character of the Bengalee people. *Bhakti* means love of God. It is a very old Hindu cult. In very ancient India, in what may be called the Vedic Age, or more accurately the *Sutra* period of Vedic history, we had this cult, where it was called *Shandilya-Vidya*; the well-known *Shandilya-Sutras* were the authoritative scripture of this old *Bhakti* cult. In the *Shandilya-Sutra*, *Bhakti* is defined as supreme devotion (lit. attachment) to the Lord or Isvara. Isvara literally means He Who directs and provides. Isvara is the Universal Providence, the Ruler and Governor of the universe. The cultivation of devotion or attachment to Him calls for the contemplation of the Lord as Providence. We receive everything from Him We have received our life, our bodily organs, our senses and their objects, our wealth and progeny—all things and persons that contribute to our happiness, from Him. The contemplation of these gifts of the Lord is the central method of the cultivation of *Bhakti* as defined in the *Shandilya-Sutra.*

This definition of *Bhakti* governed all the *Bhakti* cults of India, more or less, upto the time of Shree Chaitanya Mahapravu, the founder of Bengal Vaishnavism. Bengal Vaishnavism discovered and revealed a new type of *Bhakti* called *ragatmika* or *raganuga. Raga* means passion ; in a specific sense what may be called the sex passion, that passion which is the soul of the sex romance or the love organised in the passionate attachment between man and wife, or the hero and the heroine in literature. The cultivation of this passion in relation to the Lord is called *raganuga* or *ragatmika bhakti* by the Bengal Vaishnavas. The definition of *Bhakti* of Bengal Vaishnavism is, therefore, somewhat different from the older definition of Shandilya, and even superior to it on account of its clearer human note. This definition is the worship of the Lord, Who is the Director of all our senses, through the activity of those senses themselves. The original text runs thus :

सर्व्वोपाधि विनिर्म्मुक्तं तत्परत्वेन निर्म्मलं

हृषिकेण हृषिकेशसेवनं भक्तिरुच्यते ।

The service of the Lord of the senses through the senses is called *Bhakti.* But to warn against reducing this *Bhakti* to gross sensuousness or sensuality this definition of *Bhakti* qualifies the senses by the adjectives in the first part of this couplet, which mean that these senses must be absolutely freed from all self-regarding desires and be purified through the pursuit of the Lord alone as the Supreme Object of all sense-activities. *Bhakti* or Love of God, according to the Bengal school, must not, therefore, be identified with the pursuit of sensuality. The senses must be purified first, and they must be freed from all desire for self-enjoyment. For this object Bengal Vaishnavism has very clearly indicated the difference between lust and love. Lust in Bengalee is *kama*, and love is *prema.* The terms, however, came to be mixed up in popular imagination, wherein there was a distinct degeneration of both the words. This degeneration must have been present at the time of the birth of the Chaitanya Movement in Bengal. The two words had, therefore, to be differentiated by the Chaitanya Movement, which initiated a new *Bhakti* cult. In the Chaitanya-Charitamrita, therefore, we find *kama* or lust defined as desire for the satisfaction of one's own senses; while *prema* is defined as desire for the satisfaction of the senses of Shree Krishna.

আত্মেন্দ্রিয় প্রীতিইচ্ছা তারে বলে কাম
কৃষ্ণেন্দ্রিয় প্রীতিইচ্ছা ধরে প্রেম নাম ।

Satisfaction of the senses is an element common to both lust and love. The difference between the two is in their conscious objectives. In lust the desire for self-satisfaction or self-enjoyment dominates. In love not self-enjoyment, but the enjoyment or pleasure of the object of love overwhelms and almost obliterates the desire for self-enjoyment. This is the culmination of all love-romance. The consciousness of self is completely lost in the highest and purest love. This is common human experience. Our love, as George Elliot somewhere says, "at its highest flood loses itself in the Infinite", which means that the culmination of all true love, even in human experience, is not only the complete absence of the consciousness of self, but the realisation of the Universal in and through our particular passions. This universal human experience is really the origin of the *raganuga* cult of Bengal Vaishnavism. It is this universal human experience of the sex-passion or sex-romance that has inspired the specific definition of *Bhakti* of the Bengal school. This is the real explanation of the intensely humanistic note of the *Bhakti* cult in Bengal. It has its root in the conception of the Ultimate Reality as the Universal Man, as the highest revelation of the Divine Personality or Shree Bhagavan.

In the cultivation of this *Bhakti*, the first step is the realisation of the Absolute as the objective of all our sense-activities. The Object of the sense of sight is form or *rupam* as it is called in our language and literature. The object of the sense of hearing is sound or *shavda* ; of the sense of touch is heat and cold and softness and hardness ; of the sense of smell is odour ; of the palate is taste. *Shavda-sparsa-rupa-rasa-gandha*, – these are the objects of our five senses of audition, touch, vision, taste and smell. These constitute the fundamental elements of our sense-knowledge or perceptions

The senses and their objects are organically co-related to each other. The world of sight and our visual organ, the world of sound and our audition, the world of smell and our organ of smell, the world of taste and our palate, and the tangible world and the sense of touch,—these depend upon each other for their existence. It is impossible to conceive whether the eye existed before the evolution of the visual universe, or whether the visual universe existed before the evolution of the organ of vision. The one is absolutely dependent upon the other for its existence. This is true of all our other senses. This objective world and our senses, organised in and through our consciousness, form one organic whole. This is the logic of our sense-experience. And this logic drives us to the irresistible conclusion of the existence of Eternal and Universal Consciousness, which has held together this objective world on the one side, and our consciousness, with all our sense-organs, on the other, from eternity to eternity. This Universal Consciousness or Shree Bhagavan or Shree Krishna of the Bengal Vaishnava cult is, therefore, the root and realisation of all our sense-life and sense-activity. He is, as the Upanishads say, the Eye of our eye, the Ear of our ear, the Mind of our mind in our subjective life and experience on the one side, as He is the soul and essence of all *rupam*, all *shavda*, all *sparsa*, all *rasa* and all *gandha* on the other. These five, *shavda* etc., though organised in our material organs of audition etc, are themselves non-material or spiritual. They are called the measure (*matra*) of all material objects. These exist eternally realised and perfect in Shree Krishna, as the Object of our senses. They are organised in the Being of the Lord. Therefore, the eternal and universal objective of all our sense-organs is really not the particularities of our sense-experiences, but as objects that exist eternally realised in the very Being of the Lord Himself. This is the postulate that stands behind the definition of *Bhakti* as the worship or the service of the Lord through our senses. This is the implication of the injunction that for the realisation of this ideal of *Bhakti* the senses must be purified not by negative methods of popular mediaeval repressions and renunciations but through their idealisation and spiritualisation in the consciousness of the working and presence of Shree Bhagavan or Shree Krishna inside our sense-organs on the one hand, and in all sense-objects, on the other. This consciousness must necessarily cure all conceits of our individual ownership in our senses. It must also necessarily cure all self-regarding desires as a sin against the Lord Himself, and as suicidal to our own highest realisation of our sense-activities and sense-enjoyment as well.

The definition of *Bhakti* as the service of the Lord of the senses with the senses points to the way of *yoga* or the realisation of the presence and operation of the Lord in this world of sense-objects on the one side, and in our sense-organs on the other. This may even be the *Bhakti* of the Samkara-Vedanta school. The Samkara-Vedanteen also strives to realise the presence of Brahman in every object as well as in his senses themselves. This is the union of conciousness or *jnana-yoga*. But *Bhakti* as realised by the Bengal school is not merely the Union of Consciousness or the realisation of Brahman in all objects as well as in the senses through which we cognise them, but the Union of Love, which means the union of the devotee with the Lord in all His passions or desires and activities. This is a concrete and more complete union. This union is possible only on the plane of love. Mere consciousness of the Universal Presence of the Lord cannot bring it about, particularly as that consciousness may be the result of abstraction, the Lord Himself being realised as what is called the Abstract Universal or the *Nirguna* Brahman of our ancient theology. The union, which is the ideal of *Bhakti* or Love of God, as realised by the Bengal school, is not only the union of consciousness or *jnanam*, but also the union of passions and desires and the will of the devotee, with those of the Object of his devotion. The Lord here is conceived not as undifferentiated but as self-differentiated unity. He is constantly striving for re-integration with Himself. This is the passion of the Lord. This desire is the soul of our love also. We cannot know that which is not already in us. In all our act of knowing there is this universal fact of differentiation and integration. Similarly, in our love or passion, we do not really desire something foreign to us, but always and only that which is in our subliminal consciousness as perfect beauty. This word beauty, however, hardly exhausts the truth of love. Our word for it is *rasa*. Literally *rasa* means that which gives satisfaction and enjoyment. This *rasa* is what attracts us to things that we desire or like or love. This *rasa* is the soul and essence of what we understand as love or *prema*. The definition of *Bhakti* as

अनन्यममता विष्णौ ममता प्रेमसङ्गता

or the realisation that the Lord is mine and I am the Lord's—is fuller than the definition of *Bhakti* as the service of the Lord of the senses with the senses. In this service, the senses, cured of the conceit that they are mine, are consecrated to the Lord through contemplation of the Lord as the real owner of them. My eyes are His. He sees and enjoys His universe of *rupam* through my eyes. My ears are His. He cognises the world of sound and enjoys it through my ears. So on and so forth with regard to all our senses. This is the service of the Lord of the senses through the senses. But this is really partial union. There may not necessarily be any passion in this service of the Lord of the senses through the senses. But every act of knowledge creates or provokes some desire. Knowing and feeling are organically bound up together. Mere knowing is an abstraction. We do not know any such thing in actual experience. We may suppress the desire that follows knowing, and thereby think that knowing need not be followed by desire. That is really an abstraction. In actuality knowing must generate desire, and desire must with equal necessity prompt activity. Knowing and feeling and willing are inseparable in actual experience, though they may be conceived as separated or separable in the abstract.

These three—knowing, feeling and willing, or knowledge, emotions and will—constitute the full contents of our consciousness. These constitute the eternal elements of all consciousness. They are, or must be, present as constituent elements of the Divine Consciousness also. The Lord not only knows all, but also must desire all and must, therefore, operate upon all to shape and mould them to His desire. This is the only rational interpretation of Evolution from the theistic stand-point. This desire to evolve perfection from an imperfect world, that is constantly moving towards perfection, is the Passion of the Lord. This is the only way in which we can understand and interpret His Passion. This Passion of the Lord has its necessary counter-part in the human desire for love and perfection. This is the root of all *Bhakti* or love of the Lord. All passion means yearning for union, and the yearning of the soul for union with the Oversoul or the Lord is the very essence of *Bhakti*. This union has been realised in the cult of *Bhakti* in Bengal in a three-fold way. First, union of consciousness called *jnana-yoga* ; second, union of love or the emotions, called *bhakti-yoga* ; and third, the union of the will, called *karma-yoga*. All these three are combined in the Bengal cult of *Bhakti*. The *bhakta* or devotee, who has reached this goal, lives in perpetual consciousness of the Divine Presence. All his senses realise Him in all their objects and activities. The eye sees His *rupam* in all visible objects; the ear hears His *shavda* in every sound; and so on and so forth. The mind is possessed absolutely by thought of Him. This is the union of consciousness or *jnana-yoga*. But this consciousness of the presence of the Lord in all things and in all thoughts necessarily provoke desire or passion to enjoy Him. And this desire with equal necessity leads to the complete merging of the self of the devotee into the Self of the Divine. When this union of consciousness and the union of desire or emotion is realised, then necessarily follows the complete merging of the will of the devotee into the Will of his Deity. He works not from any self-regarding motive, but from passion for fulfilling the Will of his Lord. This is one aspect of *karma-yoga*. Another aspect of it is that the devotee, when he has attained this complete union in consciousness, in emotions and in will with his Lord, he out of sheer joy throws himself into imitating his Lord or more accurately the sport or *leela* of his Lord in his own life. In this realisation the devotee fills his whole world with the instruments of the *leela* of the Lord. His own mother becomes then the symbol of the eternally realised Motherhood of the Lord. His own father becomes the manifestation of the eternally realised Fatherhood of God. These earthly relations of ours exist eternally realised in the very Being of Bhagavan as contents of that Being. All these earthly relations become in the consciousness of the devotee representations of their eternally realised prototype in the Being of the Lord, or His manifestations here below. Father, mother, brother, sister, friend and lover, all become to the devotee, who has attained this high state of *Bhakti*, instruments and revelations of the Love of God. Social enjoyments and service thus become enjoyment and service of the Lord Himself.

In the realisations of the Bengal *Bhakti* school Bhagavan or the Lord Shree Krishna has been revealed as निखिलरसामृत मूर्त्ति, which means the eternal embodiment of all *rasa*-s.

CHAPTER III.

Art in Bengal Vaishnavism.

This concept *Nikhilarasamritamurti* or the eternal embodiment of all *rasa*-s is the soul and essence of the Vaishnavic aesthetics of Bengal. *Anandam* or bliss or joy is the soul of all art. This *anandam* is the eternal quest of art, whether of painting or sculpture or architecture or poetry or music. A synonym for this *anandam* in Hindu thought and realisation is *Rasa*. The Absolute has been described in the Upanishad as *Rasa*.

रसो वै सः

He is *rasa*.

रसह्यायम् लब्धानन्दी भवति

Through gaining this *rasa* all beings are possessed with *anandam*. Another text says that all creatures subsist on a particle of the *anandam* of Brahman or the Absolute. This *rasa* is, therefore, the soul and substance of all our enjoyment, whether material or sensuous or spiritual. And as the logic of all our enjoyments is the Absolute, the Absolute has been realised in our Vaishnavic experiences as the Eternal Embodiment of all *rasa* . He is *Nikhilarasamritamurti*.

The philosophy of art in Bengal Vaishnavism divides the *rasa*-s into two categories, namely, those that are permanent and those that are accidental. The permanent *rasa*-s are called *nitya* in Sanskrit and Bengalee. The *rasa*-s of the other class are called *agantuka* or those that come occasionally. The nine *rasa*-s of general Hindu aesthetics belong to this latter category. They are (i) *sringara*, that which is associated with the sex function; (ii) *hashya*, that which produces laughter; (iii) *advuta*, that which produces wonder; (iv) *karuna*, that which excites compassion; (v) *raudra*, that which produces awe; (vi) *bhayanaka*, that which produces fear; (vii) *vibhatsa*, that which produces disgust; (viii) *veera*, the heroic; and (ix) *shanta*, complete equanimity. These nine *rasa*-s, may also be called natural *rasa*-s. These are produced by our contact with natural objects and phenomena. They are the results of our objective experience. They are not necessarily the creation of our relations with other humans. We observe *sringara* even in the animal kingdom. And even in Nature we visualise sometimes the *raudra* or the terrible, and sometimes, as before a storm bursts, *shanta* or absolute calm, as of a flame undisturbed by a breath of wind.

Vaishnava aesthetics has realised four *rasa*-s that are produced by the romance of our human relations. These are (i) *dasya*, or the romance of the master and servitor relation, or the relation between subject and king or the romance of the filial relation ; (ii) *sakhya* or the romance of friendship ; (iii) *batsalya* or the romance of father and mother love ; and (iv) *madhurya* or the romance of the man and wife or the hero and heroine affection in literature. Though *shanta* is counted as a *rasa* in Hindu aesthetics, it is not seriously enumerated as a *rasa* in the *Bhakti* cult of Bengal, because *shanta* does not enter into any of these human relations. All romance is moved by passion, which really disturbs our equanimity. In romantic affection, whether the object of it be a king or a parent or a friend, or child or a lover, we become the sport of our passion, and lose that self-control which is the soul of equanimity or the *shanta rasa*. And as the cultivation and realisation of *bhakti* as understood by the Bengal school, involves a passionate longing for the Lord, *shanta* or equanimity has no place in it. Therefore, Bengal Vaishnavism does not count *shanta* as a constituent element of its *bhakti* or love of God. But it is nevertheless regarded as absolutely essential to the attainment of real *bhakti*, according to the realisations of Bengal Vaishnavism. As already stated, whether we accept and pursue the ideal of *bhakti* as the service of the Lord of the senses through sense-activities or as complete self-surrender to the Vishnu with supreme love, the purification of the senses, through universal God-realisation and the attainment of complete equanimity thereby, must be accepted as an absolute condition-precedent of the cultivation of *bhakti*. This is particularly necessary for the realisation of *bhakti* or love of God in and through our human relations of love and service, which is implied in the pursuit of *bhakti* through the four specific *rasa*-s, *dasya*, *sakhya*, *batsalya* and *madhura*. The apotheosis of these human relations or the complete elimination of our carnal conception regarding the objects of our love and affection as mere men and women, or, in other words, the realisation of the Absolute in all His fullness and perfection in the objects of our love aud affection,—this is a necessary pre-condition of the pursuit of this *bhakti*. And the object of the *shanta rasa*, which is acquired through Universal God-consciousness, is to prepare the ground for the cultivation of the highest *bhakti*. *Shanta*, therefore, is not regarded as a distinct *rasa* in the realisations of Vaishnavic *bhakti* in Bengal, but as the fundamental basis upon which this *bhakti* must grow.

Love of God to be real must be something concrete and personal, and not a mere abstraction or generalisation. The highest realisation of love is in what we call romance. In romantic love the physical is overwhelmed by the spiritual. Though intimately associated with our senses, when love rises to the level of romance, conciousness of the sensuous is lost in the enjoyment of that which passes beyond our senses. In fact, the senses are found in the romantic plane positive hindrances to it instead of being instruments of our enjoyment. The ultimate analysis of our realisations of love reveals the fundamental fact that even while completely giving ourselves up to the sensuous aspect of it, we really do not love the objects of our senses in our love but always, however unconsciously it may be, we hanker after and seek something which the senses can never seize. This is the soul of all romance, whether it be the romance of the *dasya* or the *sakhya* or the *batsalya* or the *madhurya* category. Every relation of master and servant or king and subject or son and father does not rise to the plane of romance. The essential characteristic of romance is the pursuit of the unseen and the ideal through the seen and real instrument of it. When the servitor loses himself completely in his master, has no desire of his own apart from the wishes of his master, or when the subject completely loses his individuality or personality in his sovereign lord and king, (as found sometimes in the feudal stage of socio-political evolution), or when the son completely loses his own personality in his father or mother, so that he has no will of his own, not only in opposition to that of parents but even apart from it, it is then and then only that our affections through these human relations rise to the plane of romance. In this romantic plane of our affections our bodies and our senses are transformed and overwhelmed by the super-sensuous and the spiritual. The servant, the subject and the son lose their outer consciousness in what may be called a trance, when in their inner consciousness they realise their absolute identity with the object of their affection. So also in the realisations of the other *rasa*-s. Our friendship does not rise to the level of *rasa* or romance in every case. Nor does our parental affections attain this ideal always. Not even is this romantic plane reached by every attachment between man and woman. In 999 cases out of every 1000 we form and follow these attachments absolutely in the carnal plane, possessed by the universal animal instincts of parental or sexual relations. Every affection or attachment between a servant and his master, a subject and his king, a son and his parent, a friend and his friend, parents and their children or between man and woman, is not romantic, does not rise to the level of *rasa*, which must be distinguished from the ordinary physical enjoyments and attachments among humans who are still on the mere animal plane. Bengal Vaishnavism, though sometimes misrepresented and misinterpreted as the pursuit of vulgar sensuality or what is called erotic in English, is really a highly spiritual culture. The sensuous and erotic interpretation of it is entirely due to the ignorance not only of outsiders but even of the Vaishnava crowd themselves of those deeper realisations verified and verifiable, upon which both Vaishnavic theology and art have been built. These realisations are, as all real realisations as distinguished from logical abstractions and philosophical generalisations, of an exceedingly complex character. In all our realisations the sensuous and the super-sensuous, the physical and the spiritual, the material and the ideal, are organically and indissolubly mixed up, like shine and shadow, as our ancients would say. All our realisations of the spiritual are really through our sense-experiences. All our realisations of God are through our direct experiences of man and this world. God as Creator cannot be abstracted from His creation. The personality of God can never be realised except in the light of our direct experiences of the human personality. We call God our Father, but the Fatherhood of God can only be realised directly by our own fatherhood. In our deepest devotions we address God as our Father, our Friend, our Lord or Lover. But these terms have their meaning and truth only in our direct experiences of the human relations. Vaishnavic *bhakti* and Vaishnavic art are both the fruit of these experiences of the human relations, which at their highest point transcend the sensuous and reach the plane of the super-sensuous or the spiritual. Purification of the senses by means of rigorous physical, psycho-physical and ethical disciplines and the exercise of that religious imagination—which is the soul of all *bhakti*—are, therefore, an essential pre-condition of the Vaishnavic *bhakti*.

The most distinguishing character of the *bhakti* cult of Bengal is what may be called its vicariousness. The cultivation of this vicarious sentiment in the pursuit of the romantic love of God or the realisation of the four *rasa*-s in relation to the Lord is necessary for the cure of all self-regarding desires in the enjoyment of these romantic experiences. This is the only way to the complete elimination of the senses and the sensuous from our actual enjoyments and exultations of the romantic affections or *rasa*-s. When Emerson wrote : "I thank ye, o young excellent lovers, ye keep the world young for me," he must have referred to this vicarious character of all selfless romance. It is not really outside even our ordinary experiences. When we enjoy the wooing of our sons and daughters and feel a resurrection of our own past youth in their romances, we realise this vicariousness. This is a common experience of all those who have been able to rise above the lowest animal plane. In these vicarious experiences there is absolutely no actual sense-reference. The cultivation of *bhakti* or love of God through the *rasa*-s of Bengal Vaishnavism is bassd upon this psychological experience. Vicariousness is a fundamental element of our enjoyment of all art-creations, whether of painting or sculpture or poetry and the drama or music. The highest form of God-realisation in the *bhakti* cult of Bengal, that which is called the *raganuga bhakti*, is really pursued through Vaishnavic art, particularly through Vaishnava lyrics or *keertana*-s. These *keertana*-s seek to portray the romance of the *Purusha* and His *Prakriti*. All the relations of life as we experience them here below, have, as already indicated, two aspects, one as eternally realised in the Being of the Lord, and the other as progressively realising in our life and experiences. These relations exist eternally realised in Shree Krishna in and through His relations with Shree Radha or His *Prakriti*. As father and son or friend and friend or as lovers, our relations here below are really reproductions of the eternally realised relations of love and romance in the Being of Shree Krishna, wherein His *Prakriti* stands as the counter-part. In seeking to cultivate the highest or *raganuga bhakti* with the help of these Vaishnava lyrics, we are distinctly asked to pursue this vicarious method. The key to the cultivation of this *bhakti* has been supplied by the Chaitanya-Charitamrita, the special scripture of Bengal Vaishnavism, in a very remarkable, though largely ignored, couplet, which says:

ब्रजे निज सिद्धदेह करिया स्मरण
निशिदिन करे राधा-कृष्णेर पूजन ।

which means that the devotee remembering his eternally realised "body" in Braja or Brindabana, day and night worships Radha-Krishna. In this eternally realised existence of ours we stand in a net-work of relations as parent and child, as friends, as lovers. And Shree Krishna and Shree Radha are the centre of this eternally realised system of relations. The Bengal Vaishnava lyrics seek to portray the sport of the Lord with His own *Prakriti* in Brindabana for the realisation of the *rasa*-s. In this drama Shree Krishna represents the son, and Yasoda represents the mother. It is worthy of notice that Shree Krishna is not born of Yasoda, but Yasoda has, so to say, *adopted* him as her son. Thus there is the essential element of vicariousness in the parental romance of Yasoda and her husband Nanda with Shree Krishna. The *dasya* romance or the romantic attachment of the servitor to his lord or master has found, however, a very small place in Bengal Vaishnava lyrics ; and there is really no representation of it in our Vaishnava *keertana*-s. These *keertana*-s are representations of the three other *rasa*-s, the *sakhya*, the *batsalya* and the *madhurya*. And this last or the *madhurya* or the romance of the man and wife or hero and heroine relation forms the principal subject of these *keertana*-s. And those who desire to pursue the ideal of romantic or *raganuga bhakti* are enjoined, while following or enjoying these *keertana*-s, to remember their eternally realised bodies, which are spiritual bodies, and their eternally realised relations, which are not carnal or sensuous but necessarily spiritual relations in the very Being of the Lord or Shree Brindabana, where everything stands in their ideal form and relation. In their eternally realised bodies they are not Shree Radha or the chief consort of Shree Krishna but are only, so to say, companions of Shree Radha. As such, they are helps to the Radha-Krishna sport, but not the principal actors. The implication is that here in their eternally realised beings in Braja or Brindabana, the devotees participate in the romantic attachment of Shree Krishna through Shree Radha vicariously and not directly.

In fact, our Vaishnavic experiences are not without parallel in the realisations of Catholic Christianity. In Christian piety, as realised by the Catholic church, the relation which the devotee seeks to realise with the Father is a vicarious relation; because he is a son through Christ by adoption. And the objective of Catholic Christian piety is to find a place by the side of the Throne of God, where sits the Son, engaged in eternal coloquy with the Father, and the highest aspiration of the Christian devotee is not to join in that coloquy himself but only to stand, in love and awe, by the Throne of the Almighty and listen to that coloquy between the Father and the Son. Similarly, the ideal-end and object of Bengal Vaishnavic piety is to merely see "the sport of the Lord with His *Prakriti*" and thus to vicariously enjoy it. To seek direct participation in the Lord's *leela*, like Shree Radha, is regarded as sin in the category of Bengal Vaishnavism. We can only enjoy His *leela* vicariously. And in this vicarious participation or enjoyment, there can possibly be no room for sense or self. Any suspicion of sense or self must inevitably destroy the essential purity and spirituality of the Bengal Vaishnava cult of *bhakti*.

This *bhakti* is the pursuit of the love of the Lord through *rasa* or *bhava* or the emotions. And it is clearly laid down in the very first aphorism of the scripture of aesthetics or *rasa* of Bengal Vaishnavism that

निर्व्विकारात्मके चित्ते भाव: प्रथम विकारः।

The mind must be completely cured of all sensuous attachments or sense-quickening to generate *rasa* or romance or what is called *bhava* here or the emotion. The test of the purity of the mind is the absence of all manner of sense-quickening even in the presence of the objects of the senses before the senses and through them before the mind. This purity can only be attained by what is called the vicarious method of idealisation and spiritualisation. Those who know or understand these fundamentals of the Art of Bengal Vaishnavism cannot, therefore, charge it with eroticism.

In fact, even in the ordinary experiences of sex passion, if only we minutely analyse them, we find that though it originates in our sex activities, it always strives to transcend these activities. As long as we have not been able to do so, our sex-love does not and cannot rise to the level of the romantic.

The body is not the objective of this passion. The whole being hungers after complete union with that of the object of our love. And as in our present life we are not mere spirit or soul, but our spirit or soul is indissolubly bound up with our body, being influenced by it and influencing it, we cannot in actual realisation completely eliminate our body from this hunger for complete union. But though we cannot absolutely negate our physical organs and instruments in the realisation of the highest romantic affection, we always strive to rise above the limitations of these in our desire for the complete union. Our Vaishnava lyrics have repeatedly essayed to present this yearning of love to eliminate, so far as may be, the limitations of the flesh in its passionate desire for union with its lover. And the key to this realisation is not abstraction of the spiritual from the physical, but the idealisation and spiritualisation of the latter. Realism and idealism have, therefore, been exquisitely blended together in the Vaishnavic cult and culture of Bengal in all its three essential aspects, in its philosophy, its religion, and its art.

The Art of Bengal Vaishnavism is embodied in the Bengalee Vaishnavic lyrics. These are to the Vaishnava devotees at once both their art and religion, both their poetry and their scripture. These lyrics are sung during their devotional exercises, as it is through these lyrics that the Vaishnava devotees of Bengal seek to realise vicariously the supreme love of Radha and Krishna or Bhagavan and His *Prakriti.* The Rhada-Krishna *leela* is the soul and centre of these Vaishnava lyrics. Though they present the three dominant *rasa*-s, namely, *sakhya* or the romance of friendship, *batsalya* or the romance of parent love, and *madhurya* or the romance of sex relation, the last dominates the other two. And in all these Shree Krishna is the soul and centre. In *sakhya* the cowherds of Brindabana move round Shree Krishna as the common object of their romance. It is He Who leads them in their sport in the pasture fields, where they all follow Him with their cattle. It is again He Who is the soul and centre of the romance of parent-love in these lyrics, where Yasoda plays the part of the mother, and combines in her really the entire motherhood of Brindabana. The mothers of the youthful cowherds, the playmates of Shree Krishna, all find in Yasoda and Shree Krishna a representation of their own mother-love. In fact, the Bengal poets have universalised this romance of mother-love by making the boy Shree Krishna the object not only of the mother-love of Yasoda and the whole mother-folk of Brindabana, but even of the animal kingdom. When Shree Krishna and the other cowherds lead their cattle to the pasture, even the cows in the herd are made to cast their entranced look on Shree Krishna and lick His limbs in rapture as they do in the case of their own calves, and while they do so milk spurts out spontaneously of their udders indicating a blending of the physical and the non-physical or the spiritual, if we may say so. This, I think, has absolutely no parallel in any literature. These Vaishnava lyrics relating to mother-love or *batsalya* are a picture not of any particular romance of the parental affection, but of the universal parent-love. As we read these or hear them sung in *keertana*-s, we vicariously realise and enjoy this exquisite presentation of the ideal of parent-love or *batsalya*, where body and soul are blended together. So also in the presentation of the romance of friendship. As we read or listen to these lyrics, we actually re-live our own youths, and thus vicariously realise the emotions of our youthful friendships.

But the special feature of these Vaishnava lyrics is their unconscious reference to the sex romance, wherein all these episodes, either of *sakhya* or of *batsalya*, are made to culminate and find their highest and final self-fulfilment. Because the object of all these is really to quicken the romantic love of the devotee for his Deity, the cultivation of this sentiment vicariously through the contemplation of the eternal love-sport of Shree Krishna with His *Prakriti* is the soul and essence of the Vaishnavic *bhakti* cult in Bengal. And though Shree Radha is this *Prakriti* in a specific sense, all the *Gopinees*, whether they are mothers or wives, as well as the youths and playmates of Shree Krishna in Brindabana, are really included in Shree Radha—are manifestations of Shree Radha on different planes of our many-sided romantic relations. In fact, psychologically or more correctly perhaps psycho-physically, all the romances of human relations have, however unconsciously or subconsciously, a universal sex reference. There is this sex reference, however unconscious we may be of it and however shocked we may feel at the mere mention of it, even in the other three *rasa*-s, the *dasya*, the *sakhya*, and the *batsalya* of our Vaishnavic aesthetics. The *dasya rasa* or the romance of the servitor and master relation is different from and must not be identified with even the most loyal attachment of the servant to his master and of the complete subordination of the wishes and will of the former to those of the latter. The test of romance is the complete transfiguration of the servitor, both physically or in his nervous system and emotionally or spiritually, during his service. When the servant falls into a trance and loses all outer consciousness in an onrush of ecstacy at the touch of his master's body or even at the sight of him, it is then and then only that the servitor relation rises to the plane of the romantic, and loses all taint not only of the physical but even of those degrading social distinctions that ordinarily constitute this relation. The servitor is no more conscious of the dignity and superiority of his master's position than of the indignity and inferiority of his own position. He and his master become completely identified in the beatific consciousness of this romance. In this romance, when it is organised in the relation between the son and the father, the same thing happens, as it did in the case of Christ, who in his beatitude declared : "I and my Father are one". Christ did not desire here to bring the Father down to his own level, nor raise himself to the level of the Father, but only proclaim a fact of his deepest realisation of the romance of the son and father love, wherein the sense of all difference of status is completely lost in the consciousness of that unity or identity with the object of his love, which is the eternal hankering of all romantic affection. It is only when this highest beatitude is attained, that the servitor and master or the son and father relation rises to the level of *rasa* or romance. Unless and until this is achieved, *dasya* remains, what it generally is, a mere physical or social relation, and does not acquire the spiritual quality of *rasa* or romance. The same remark applies to father or mother love also. Men and women may love their progeny even to distraction. They may consecrate themselves to the ceaseless and untiring service of their children. But these alone do not raise their carnal affections for their progeny to the level of the romantic. Here also the real test of *rasa* is the physical or psycho-physical transfiguration of their whole being, body and soul together, into the universal form of parent-love or *batsalya*. When this real romantic stage is reached, the physical in the mother loses itself in the spiritual, and the spiritual or the universal manifests itself in the particularities of the mother's physical, psycho-physical, mental and emotional constitution. All the physical manifestations of mother-love appear, when this stage is reached, even when its object is not present before the mother's senses. Similarly, the same remark applies equally to the *madhurya* or the romance of the man and woman relation. Every relation of the sexes is not *madhurya*. Every sex relation does not rise to the level of *rasa* or the romantic, however exulting or passionate the experience of it may be. There is a natural exultation and even a passionate longing for losing one's self, body and spirit—all, in the union with the object of one's sex passion. This is no uncommon experience. Absolute purification of the senses or their idealisation is not essential for the attainment of this experience. But this very common physical experience is no proof of the elevation of the ordinary animal sex passion to the plane of the spiritual and the romantic. This is no proof that the sex passion has been elevated to the plane of *rasa* or romance. The first evidence of it is that the exultation of the sex enjoyment is not followed by the almost universal physical or psycho-physical depression, when with satiation both body and mind turn away from the object of the sex passion. But this is not all. The whole experience must be universalised and spiritualised. When the physical drops off like the yellow leaves of autumn, and the emotional and the spiritual overwhelm the whole being of the lover, it is then and then only that sex-love reaches the truly romantic plane.

The four *rasa*-s of our Vaishnava aesthetics are deduced from the actual realisations of different kinds of devotees. Some, by the very make and nature of their being, find their highest self-fulfilment in the cultivation of the *dasya rasa.* This is the predominant note, for instance, in the Judaic or Moslem piety, where the Ultimate Reality has been apprehended primarily as the "Lord Almighty". In fact, in the earliest Hebrew records, we find no mention of the love of God, but only reference to His might and majesty. God has been worshipped both in Judaism and Islam only as the abode of all might and the source of all law and justice. He is the King, the earth is His kingdom, mankind are His subjects. This is the predominant God-idea in both Judaism and Islam. Therefore, those brought up under the influence of these two world-religions naturally cultivate the *dasya* form of piety. When, however, Judaism came in contact with Greek thought and culture, a new dispensation was ordained in Christianity. The earlier Judaic piety started a new course of evolution. The older vehicle of this piety was the king and subject relation. The new idea in Christianity was the Fatherhood of God, and the son and father relation became the vehicle of Christian love for the Lord. It was not very different from the older idea, only the new relation became far more intimate than the old king and subject relation. In Islam the older Judaic ideal prevailed, while the Christian ideal of father and son was openly repudiated as ascribing an anthropomorphic conception to the Deity. But Judaism, Christianity and Islam are fundamentally one in the ideal of their piety, which would be classed by Bengal Vaishnavic thought as belonging to the *dasya* plane. But both Christianity and Islam reached, or more correctly perhaps approached, the *sakhya* plane in the life and experiences of their saints and seers, some of whom, as for instance Madame Guyon of the

French Catholic church, touched even the highest *madhurya* plane or piety or *bhakti* of the Bengal classification. But these lack, strictly speaking, the reality of our Vaishnavic realisations.

Bengal Vaishnavism, however, recognises in all these a very high class of piety. Each of these four *rasa*-s have been described as the best and highest for those who cultivate them severally, following their inner nature and constitution. Some are constitutionally fitted for the cultivation of the servitor and master relation, or the son and father relation, or the subject and king relation ; some are, by the very make and constitution of their being, best equipped for the pursuit of the *sakhya bhakti* or the cultivation of piety or love of God in and through the romance of friendship; others are equally fitted for the cultivation of the romance of parent love in relation to the Divine; while others, and their number is exceedingly small, are qualified by the constitution of their mind and soul for the pursuit of the *madhurya bhakti* or the realisation of the love of God in and through the romance of the man and woman or the hero and heroine relation. These four types of piety are each best and highest for those who are fitted by nature for their cultivation. But judged absolutely and without relation to the needs and capacity of individual devotees, *madhurya* or the romance of the man and woman or the hero and heroine relation is the highest form of Vaishnavic piety. Because, in this romance there is a combination of the essential qualities of all the other *rasa*-s. In the *sringara* or the sex romance there is the romance of service, which is the soul of the *dasya rasa*. There is also in it the romance of friendship, which adds a new feature or quality to the *dasya* romance, namely, that of the sense of absolute equality. In it there is also the romance of *batsalya*, which combines in it the essentials of the *dasya* and the *sakhya*, adding to these a new element, namely, that of protective care. All these, namely, selfless service, absolute equality and protective care, are essential elements of the sex romance. But there is a new element in it, the element of passionate hankering for complete unification or identification of one's self with the object of one's romance, wherein both body and soul seek and find their highest self-realisation in and through the self-realisation its own object. For this reason Bengal Vaishnavism, while fully and frankly recognising the value of all forms of *bhakti* or love of God, gives the highest place to what is called the *madhurya* or the sex romance. The Chaitanya-Charitamrita declares that the object of the advent of Shree Chaitanya Mahaprabhu is to initiate a new *bhakti* movement ; this new *bhakti* had never been revealed or practised before.

The central idea of the Vaishnavic art of Bengal is derived or developed from its conception of the five *rasa*-s, *shanta*, *dasya*, *sakhya*, *batsalya* and *madhura*. These *rasa*-s are not mere abstractions or generalisations, but they are concrete things. They are not what is called formless or *nirakara*, but all these *rasa*-s have their specific forms. The object of all art is to bring out the specific forms of the different *rasa*-s. In painting, the forms of different *rasa*-s are sought to be brought out through combination of colours ; in sculpture through organisation of muscles and contour ; in poetry through representation with the help of words ; in music through sound ; in dancing through movement of living limbs. The aim and object of Vaishnavic lyrics have been to bring out, with the help of verbal description, the essential *forms* of the different *rasa*-s. These forms, though manifested in and through our bodies, are really not physical, but spiritual. The expression is, no doubt, physical. But the substance or reality that produces these expressions is really spiritual. The nine natural *rasa*-s, laughter, wonder, etc. have their meaning not really in themselves but in their relation to human emotions. Nature, according to the Bengal Vaishnavic aesthetics, is, therefore, regarded as help and accessory to the *rasa*-s. It has no independent basis of *rasa*. The entire system of Vaishnavic *rasa* or aesthetics, therefore, centres around man and his emotions and enjoyment derived from his relation with other humans. We have exquisite portrayal of what is called the beauty of Nature in Vaishnavic lyrics. But they have all reference to the human actors on the stage of which Nature finds the setting. There is, therefore, no delineation of abstract beauty or grandeur of Nature in Vaishnavic lyrics. Our Vaishnavic thought realised goodness through good men and women only, and not as a generalisation or abstraction from the concrete goodness of real men and women. So also with regard to beauty. There is no such thing as the beautiful in the conception of our Vaishnavic thought ; it is always the beautiful person who represents the reality of what we call beautiful. And Shree Krishna or the Ultimate Reality is, therefore, not the Beautiful of European philosophy, but *Rasamritamurti*, the eternal embodiment of all *rasa* or romance. This concept *Nikhila-rasamritamurti* sums up not only the entire philosophy of our Vaishnavic art but also the deepest and the highest realisation of the Vaishnava piety of Bengal. It is this which distinguishes Bengal Vaishnavism among the many Vaishnavic schools of mediaeval India.

CHAPTER IV.

Bengal Vaishnava Lyrics.

The hymnology of Bengal Vaishnavism goes under the general name of *keertana*. These *keertana*-s stand divided into two classes. One is called *nama-keertana*, which means the chanting of the name of the Lord. The repetition of the name of the Lord with every incoming and outgoing breath is an essential discipline of the *bhakti* cult of Bengal. This is not peculiar to Bengal Vaishnavism. This is our inheritance from Buddhism. In the Geeta it is called *japa-yajna*. *Yajna* has been, though somewhat loosely, rendered into English as 'sacrifice.' And the Geeta says that this *japa-yajna* is much superior to the *yajna* or sacrifice wherein material objects are offered to the Deity. The superiority of this *japa-yajna* over the sacrifice of material objects consists in its essentially mental character. The name of the Lord has to be repeated incessantly with a view to help the concentration of the mind upon the Lord. The name of the Lord is not a mere meaningless word. It represents the thing for which every name stands. And while repeating the name of the Lord the devotee has to concentrate his mind upon what may be called the attributes of the Lord. This is the real meaning and purpose of what is called *nama-keertana* in the literature of Bengal Vaishnavism. In *nama-keertana* the name of the Lord is joined to the psycho-physical exercise called *pranayama*, which may be generally explained as regulation of the breath. This regulation of the breath or *pranayama* is a common Hindu discipline. Its object is to quicken our nerve-centres and thereby help the concentration of the mind on the object of worship at the same time awakening that religious imagination through which all devotional feelings flow. Our Vaishnavic *nama-keertana*-s have their meaning and purpose in this; they help to concentrate the mind upon the Lord through repetition of His name, and through the psycho-physical exercise called *pranayama* or regulation of the breath, which is an essential element in all vocal music. These *keertana*-s help to quicken the devotional feelings which naturally flow from the contemplation of the Lord. These *nama-keertana*-s help the devotee to completely lose himself in the consciousness of the Lord, which is in the first stages a subjective experience only; but gradually it possesses even the outer senses, thereby filling not only the inner consciousness of the devotee with the Presence of the Deity but also covering his outer sense-contacts with the Divine Presence. These *nama-keertana*-s gradually possessing both the inner consciousness and the outer sense-contacts of the devotee with the Presence of the Divine result in that state of trance wherein he sees even with his outer eye his Lord. This experience has been recorded in the literature of Bengal Vaishnavism by the familiar statement :

स्थावर जङ्गम देखे देखे ना तार मूर्त्ति
यांहा नेत्र पड़े तांहा इष्टदेवस्फूर्त्ति ।

The devotee (in this state) no doubt sees both objects that move not and those that move, but wherever his eyes fall there is the manifestation of his God. It means, that the *rupam* or the form of the Lord covers to the eye of the devotee all visible objects. He sees the flowering bushes in his garden, he sees the cattle in his field, he sees the horses passing by his road, he sees men, women and children moving about him,—but all these outer sights are covered with the reflection of the spiritual halo of the Lord. The earth, with all things stationery or moving upon it, assumes a weird appearance covered with a light not belonging to earth or heaven, that captivates his whole being, both sensuous and spiritual, and gradually reveals in a concrete form the Presence of the Lord Himself. To the Vaishnava this Presence is necessarily that of Shree Krishna. To the Christian, when he attains this state, the experience is embodied not in the presence of Shree Krishna but of the Christ. To the Buddhist the same experience is revealed through the familiar form of the Lord Buddha. It will thus be seen that the psychology of the Vaishnavic beatitude is nothing peculiar to Vaishnavism, but is the common psychology of the beatific experiences of all religions. This experience is neither entirely subjective nor absolutely objective, but the subjective and the objective mingle together in it. The ultimate result following the ecstatic repetition or chanting of the name of the Lord is this beatific experience, which is marked by a supreme exultation of both mind and body. This exultation produces those psycho-physical transformations that go by the general name of *satvikee vikara*, (literally spiritual transformations) that are manifested on the physical or physiological plane in (i) perspiration, (ii) tremor, (iii) *pulaka*, which means that extreme exultation of the nerves that lead to the hair of body to stand erect, (iv) flowing of tears, (v) pallor, (vi) unsteady voice, (vii) absolute stillness of the body, and (viii) trance or swoon, wherein all outer consciousness is lost.

These transformations result both from the chanting of the name of the Lord or *nama-keertana* and the singing of lyrics depicting the *leela* or sport of the Lord, or what goes by the generic name of *rasa-keertana*. Every one can pursue the worship of the Lord through *nama-keertana*, but those whose senses have not been purified by means of strict and laborious physical, psycho-physical, mental, ethical and spiritual disciplines are not entitled to adopt the exercises of the *rasa-keertana*. These *rasa-keertana*-s, organised in the Bengal Vaishnava lyrics, that paint the romance of the different emotions, have a dual aspect : one sensuous and even erotic, and the other super-sensuous and spiritual. Those who are not trained to idealise and spiritualise their human and sensuous relations are not qualified to really enjoy and spiritually profit by the *rasa-keertana*-s, that paint in the terms of vulgar carnal experiences the beatitudes of the soul that completely abandons itself to the contemplation and enjoyment of the romantic sports of the Lord. To the un-illumined and the impure these Vaishnava lyrics inevitably seem to be erotic. And this is the real cause of the undoubted degeneration into which the Vaishnava lyrics have fallen at the hands of the carnal crowd.

But even apart from their highly esoteric and spiritual character, these lyrics, judged even by ordinary canons of art and psychology, do not justify the vulgar use and interpretation to which they have been reduced by the impure and un-illumined crowd, both inside the Vaishnava cult and outside it. In fact, these Vaishnava lyrics are not all of the same class or character. The majority of the later compositions are really imitations of the earlier masters, particularly of the music of their sound than of the truth of their experiences or realisations.

The real spiritual significance of the Vaishnava lyrics depicting the psycho-physical transformations brought about by ecstatic emotions lies in what has been described as ***satvikee vikara***. ***Vikara*** means literally a change from the normal state. The eight kinds of transformations, namely, profuse perspiration, tremor etc. are a common chracteristic of extreme sensuous excitement, particularly of the sex passion. The mere manifestation of these transformations are not spiritual, and therefore they do not prove the highest exultation of *bhakti* or love of the Lord. When these transformations appear in a person without the presence of any sense-object, they are called *satvikee vikara* or spiritual transformations. The absence of sense-objects raises these workings even on the physical plane to the spiritual level. It is therefore and with a view to distinguish these from the familiar concomitants of sex excitement or sense-excitement that these transformations are styled as *satvikee* or spiritual. The nervousness and emotional exultation is common to both the sensuous and the spiritual manifestations. It is only in the beatitudes of the lover of God or *bhakta* that these very physical and psycho-physical transformations are characterised as *satvikee*. The test of the spiritual character of these transformations is in the purity of the senses and the mind of the devotee.

But even here imagination plays a very great and vital part, introducing these spiritual transformations. *Bhakti* or love of God must be what is called *ahaitukee*, which means without any normal or familiar cause, such as contemplation of the mercy or benign providence of the Lord. Just as a thing of beauty, whether in Nature or in men or women, by its mere presence attracts the mind and excites a passionate longing for its possession and enjoyment, even so in *ahaitukee bhakti* or the love of the Lord not quickened by any extraneous cause, the mere consciousness of the Divine Presence or the revelation of His Beauty captivates both our outer senses and inner consciousness. This *ahaitukee bhakti* is a special realisation of Bengal Vaishnavism, which has described the Lord not only as a Person with a form—not material like ours but spiritual—but as the eternal embodiment of all joy and bliss—*Nikhilarasamritamurti*. The Upanishads described Brahman as *rasa* and *anandam*. Our Vaishnava realisations have discovered an eternally realised form or *murti* of Brahman, and have, therefore, described the Ultimate Reality as *Nikhilarasamritamurti*.

We are able to understand what this beatific realisation of the Vaishnavic piety of Bengal means, though indirectly, from our experiences of the dramatic art. In drama we visualise what may be called the forms or *murti* of the different emotions. Thc sex passion, for instance, is presented on the stage through certain transformations in the body of the actors, in their muscles, particularly of the face. These muscular transformations indicat e the *form* of the sex life. These transformations, as we see them on the stage, are, however, always tentative. They do not completely reveal the full and perfected form of the sex romance but only suggest it. These representations on the stage by their suggestiveness reveal to our mind and imagination what the *perfected form* of the sex love or the sex romance must bc. So also with regard to the other emotions or *rasa*-s. On the stage, if and where the dramatic art has reached a very high state of perfection, we are able, similarly, to visualise in the very physical transformations of the actors or actresses representing the other *rasa*-s, namely, that of the romance of friendship or the romance of parental affection or the romance of loyal service or filial love, the form of these *rasa*-s. Those who have seen a mother, nursing her child with her whole mind and body, transformed with mother-love, can somewhat understand what is meant by the form of parent-love. The picture of the Madonna has tried to bring this form out. By referring to these experiences of the dramatic art or of painting or sculpture we are able to conceive what the *murti* or body of the different emotions or *rasa*-s are.

Our Vaishnava beatitudes refer to the Lord or Brahman in His concrete revelations not as without form or body but as *Nikhila-rasamritamurti*, or the eternally realised embodiment of all *rasa*. The vision of the Lord, therefore, by its eternally realised beauty attracts not only the mind but through the mind even the outer senses of the devotee. This attraction is not produced by anything extraneous. It is not the result of the thought of the goodness or mercy or providence of the Lord. *Bhakti* produced by these considerations is not *ahaitukee* or spontaneous. This latter type of *bhakti* is the product of the direct vision of the Lord in all His Beauty and Perfection. When the devotee is blessed with this beatific vision, it produces in his outer body and senses transformations similar to those that are commonly observed in the highest exultations of our mind and body through sense or sex-contact. The former transformations are described in the literature of Bengal *bhakti* as *satvikee vikara* or spiritual transformations. These, namely, perspiration, tremor, etc. are produced during both *nama-keertana* and *rasa-keertana* in Vaishnava *bhaktas*, who have attained a high state of spirituality, whose senses have been purified and whose mind and the representative faculty have been habituated to realise the super-sensuous in the sensuous. The key to the interpretation of the concept *Nikhila-rasamritamurti* must be sought and found in the realisations and revelations of this highly developed type of Vaishnava *bhakti*.

The Bengal Vaishnava lyrics have pictured with exquisite finesee all the shades and degrees of intensity of the various romances. All romance is born of direct personal contact or realisation. Imagination does not produce really the forms of the *absolutely* unknown. Shakespeare's definition of poetry which says, "As imagination bodies forth the forms of things unknown, the poet's pen turns them into shape and gives to airy nothing a local habitation and a name", does not, therefore, really apply to our Vaishnavic lyrics. They are not works of fancy, but of true imagination, which does not create something out of nothing but always follows our direct sense-experiences to their super-sensuous or spiritual suggestions and thus builds forms of things unknown, as we loosely call them, out of the forms of things that are known. The result of it is that in our Vaishnava lyrics the sensuous and the super-sensuous or the physical and the spiritual are indissolubly and organically bound up. To the un-illumined crowd, therefore, these lyrics appeal through their sense-reference, while to the illumined saints and devotees they represent the eternally realised sport or *leela* of the Lord.

There are two classes of these lyrics, representing the two main states or experiences of our romantic affections. One class represents these experiences when the object of these romances is not present to the enjoyer or subject. These romances originate in either the direct vision of the object or in the indirect knowledge of the object communicated through some description of the object, or in the vision of the object in dream or in some picture or painting. In all these there is always a passionate longing for union with the object of the romance. This passion develops through what are called ten stages : (i) *lalasha* or the desire for enjoyment ; (ii) *udvega*, anxiety due to the sense of uncertainty whether the desire will be fulfilled or not; (iii) *jagarya* or sleeplessness; (iv) *tanava*, physical emaciation; (v) *jadima*, loss of physical activity; (vi) *vyagram*, extreme eagerness; (vii) *vyadhi*, disease, particularly of the hysteric type; (viii) *unmada*, madness; (ix) *moha*, coma; and (x) *mrityu*, death. These ten stages mark the state of separation from the object of the romance. The other class paints the various moods of exultation during the union of the object of the romance with the enjoyer or subject. In both these the common element is the passion for union, which indicates the true character of the romance and helps to bring out the almost infinite moods of the romantic passion. The soul of this passion has been revealed in a remarkable confession of Shree Radha, which says:

"सखि कि पुछसि अनुभव मोय
सोइ पीरिति अनुराग बाखानिते
तिले तिले नूतन होय।
जनम अवधि हाम मो रूप नेहारलु'
नयन ना तिरपित भेल।
लाख लाख युग हाम हिये हिय राखलु'
तबु हिय जुड़न ना गेल।"

"You ask me, dear, of my realisations of that love and attachment. How shall I describe it? It becomes new from moment to moment. From my birth have my eyes fed upon the beauty of his body and form, but they are not yet satisfied. For countless æons has my heart pressed to itself his heart, yet the burning passion of it has not been cooled."

But though, generally speaking, our Vaishnava lyrics have been divided into these two classes, the song of separation and the song of union, at their final analysis, they are all directly or indirectly inspired by the pang of separation, which is present even in the closest union. This union is never absolute or complete. The physical union may be so, but the closest physical contact leaves the yearning of the soul for union with the soul untouched. Another lyric says:

एमन पोरिति कभु देखि नाइ शुनि ।
निमिखे मानये युग, कोड़े दूर मानि ॥
समुखे राखिया करे बसनेर बा ।
मुख फिराइले तार भये कांपे गा ॥
एकतनु हैया दोंहे रजनी गोंयाय ।
सुखेर सागरे डुबि अवधि ना पाय ॥
रजनी प्रभात हइले कातर हियाय ।
देह छाड़ि येन प्राण दूरे चलि याय ॥

"None has seen or heard of such attachment!

To it the twinkling of an eye seems like an æon, and the closest embrace seems as the widest separation. Setting her before him he fans her with his scarf, but at the slightest turning of her face his whole body trembles with fear. These two spend the whole night as one body, drowned in the bottomless ocean of bliss. At break of day with drooping heart life seems to fly far away from the body."

In another lyric even a deeper strain has been struck. It paints the eternal presence of the pang of separation even in the keenest ecstacy of union.

एमन पीरिति कभु देखि नाइ शुनि ।
पराणे पराण बांधा आपनि आपनि ॥
दुँहु कोड़े दुँहु काँदे बिच्छेद भाबिया ।
तिल आध ना देखिले जाय ये मरिया ॥

"None has seen or heard of such attachment ! Their souls are knit together by themselves. Locked in each other's embrace they weep at the thought of separation. They die if they cannot see each other for half a moment."

In both union and separation this yearning for closer and closer union and the passion for enjoyment create a perpetual tragedy. This tragic note is the soul of the Vaishnava lyrics of Bengal, and it is an evidence of their essentially spiritual character, their grossest physical delineations notwithstanding. This is why these lyrics of our Vaishnava *rasa-keertana* have found exquisite instruments for the cultivation of that peculiar type of piety or *bhakti* called *raganuga*, characterised by the romantic passion of the devotee for his Lord. The un-illumined crowd find in these lyrics only a representation of the familiar sex passion. The more refined interpret these as symbolic of the relation between the human soul and the Oversoul. But they too are mere "worshippers at the gate" of the temple of our Vaishnavic *bhakti*. But those who are posted in the philosophy of the Absolute of Bengal Vaishnavism and are able to conceive of the Lord as *Nikhilarasamritamurti* or the eternal embodiment of all *rasa* or romance, are able, if not to directly realise this *raganuga bhakti*, at least to understand and appreciate its rationale and truth. They are able to realise the great injustice which unimaginative and unspiritual ignorance has done to our Vaishnavic art and piety by putting sensual and erotic meaning on these.

The highest expression of this *bhakti* is found in the lyrics of complete surrender that occur in the drama of the romantic love of

Radha and Krishna, when after separation the two find themselves united. These are called *atma-nivedanam*, literally self-consecration. These lyrics have been used in the devotional exercises even of the extremely Puritanic school of the Brahmo Samaj. One of these runs thus :

बँधु कि आर बलिब आमि।
मरणे जीवने जनमे जनमे
प्राणनाथ हैयो तुमि॥
तोमार चरणे आमार पराणे
बाँधिल प्रेमेर फाँसि।
सब समर्पिया एकमन हैया
निश्चय हइलाम दासी॥
भाविया छिलाम ए तिन भुवने
आर मोर केह आछे।
राधा बलि केह शुधाइते नाइ
दाँड़ाब काहार काछे॥

"What more shall I say, Dearest! In death and life, from life to life, be Thou my Lord and Soul. I have tied my soul to Thy feet in a love-knot; Surrendering everything, with one mind and heart, I have dedicated myself to Thy service. I fancied that in all the three worlds I had some one to call my own; but there is none to seek me and call me by my name, Radha; by whom then shall I stand?"

In another lyric Shree Radha in her supreme consecration to her Lord Shree Krishna reaches the state of that highest beatitude wherein all distinctions of both good and evil are lost. Here she says:

बँधु तुमि से आमार प्राण।
देह मन आदि तोँमारि सँपेछि
कुलशील जाति मान॥
* * * * *
पारिति-रसेते ढालि तनु मन
दियाछि तोमार पाय।
तुमि मोर पति, तुमि मोर गति
मन नाहि आन भाय॥
कलङ्की बलिया डाके सब लोके
ताहाते नाहिक दुख।
तोमार लागिया कलङ्केर हार
गलाय परिते सुख॥
सती बा असती तोमाते विदित
भाल मन्द नाहि जानि।
कहे चण्डीदास पाप पुण्य सम
तोहारि चरणखानि॥

"Dearest! Thou art my life. To Thee have I surrendered my body and mind, my birth and my honour. Immersing my limbs and my thoughts in Thy love have I consecrated them at Thy feet. Thou art my Lord. Thou art my Destiny ; nothing else appeals to my mind. People call me fallen, I do not grieve at it. To put on for Thee the necklace of evil fame is my greatest happiness. Loyal or disloyal, Thou knowest all. I know not good or evil. At They feet, (says Chandidas) sin and virtue are both the same."

This is the highest state of God-consciousness, which is, in the language of Neitzche, "beyond both good and evil".

Many of these lyrics of Bengal Vaishnavism are really pictures of spiritual endeavours. The inner meaning and significance of these can only be unlocked by the key of practical *sadhana* or spiritual culture. The poems of Chandidas start with a remarkable lyric saying :

सइ, केबा शुनाइले श्याम नाम ।
कानेर भितर दिया मरमे पशिल गो
आकुल करिल मोर प्राण ॥
ना जानि कतेक मधु श्याम नामे आछे गो
बदन छाड़िते नाहि पारे ।
जपिते जपिते नाम अवश करिल गो
के मने पाइब सइ तारे ॥

Addressing her boon companion, Shree Radha here evidently describes her experiences following upon her initiation, which consists of the communication of the name of the Lord by the *guru* to the disciple. The *guru* here is not the *guru* of the family tradition, but the *guru* who, having realised in his own consciousness and experience the beatitudes of the deepest spiritual life and aquired in consequence high psychic powers, is able to reproduce some of these experiences through his hypnotic influence in the disciple. "Friend, What is this name, Shyama, (Shyama is a name of Shree Krishna) that has been communicated to me? It has entered into my soul through my ear, and has stirred to its depths my whole being. I know not what sweetness (literally nectar) is contained in the name Shyama; my tongue cannot leave it. Repeating this name (with every breath) I lose control of my senses. How shall I, Friend, find Him?"

This is a common experience of our Vaishnavic initiation. In this initiation the *guru* communicates the name of the Lord to the disciple, and when the *guru* is an adept, who has acquired the vision of the Lord, the communication of this name to the disciple produces the results described here. The disciple's senses and thoughts are immediately captured by the sweetness of this name, and he commences to repeat it automatically with every incoming and outgoing breath. He continues to do so even during his sleep, so that this mental repetition of the name of the Lord is the first thing of which he becomes conscious after he awakes. This produces a kind of intoxication, and though living and moving in the sensuous world about him, he is possessed by the vision of something which the senses cannot seize. This produces an intense yearning in him for the direct and concrete realisation of the Lord. The experience, however, does not last long. It cannot possibly do so. Because, it is produced by the hypnotic spell of the master; and when this intoxication passes away, it leaves behind it a foretaste of the highest beatitude and thus leads the novice to throw himself with all his body and soul into those physical, psycho-physical, ethical and spiritual exercises that lead to the highest realisations. In those lyrics that describe the first stage of the romance of Shree Radha and Shree Krishna, our Vaishnava poets have recorded these spiritual endeavours. In one of these we read :

आगो राधार कि हलो अन्तरे व्यथा ।

बसिया बिरले थाकइ एकले
ना शुने काहार कथा ॥
सदाइ धेयाने चाहे मेघ-पाने
ना चले नयनेर तारा ।
बिरति आहारे राङ्गा बास परे
येमत योगिनो पारा ॥

"What pain has entered into the heart of Shree Radha? She avoids the company of her associates; sits by herself and does not exchange a word with any. Lost in contemplation she always looks at the clouds; the pupils of her eyes do not move. She has no liking for her food; and she affects the ochre-coloured garment of the *yogee.*"

All these are really a description of the early stages of religious and spiritual endeavours.

The ten stages that mark, according to Bengal Vaishnavic aesthetics, the progress of the romantic passion referred to above, namely, longing, anxiety etc., ending with insanity, coma and death, are really stages of the evolution of the highest love of the Lord. Insanity, coma and death are not here the physical ailments and conditions with which we are familiar. In fact, the mystery of madness has not as yet been completely solved. Ordinarily, the sign of madness is the absence of the consciousness of the natural relation between our perceptions and their objects. The mad man sees visions that do not correspond to the actualities of the sights present to the eye. He hears sounds which are not objectively present to the ear. He peoples the world about him with objects and persons not cognisable by our outer senses. These are the common evidences of what we understand as insanity. The devotee also in his deepest beatitude lives, moves and has his being in a world of the super-sensuous or the spiritual. He sees visions and hears sounds or music and even smells odours that have no relation to any sense-object. These visions are spiritual visions. The sound, the odour, are all what may be called spiritual. The devotee lives during these trances in a world of his own. This is the insanity referred to in our Vaishnavic aesthetics as a state of the romantic passion. This is followed by coma, which is really not an unconscious state, but what may be called a super-conscious condition. Death here is also not physical death but the complete cutting off of the channel of the outer consciousness, the channel that establishes and helps to continue the communication between the self, through the mind and the senses, and the objective world about us. It is called *samadhi* in our spiritual literature. This *samadhi* may be either only partial or absolutely complete. When it is partial, the devotee loses only outer consciousness. When it is complete, there is cessation of the functioning even of the inner organs; the lungs do not breathe, the heart does not beat. In this state of profound *samadhi*, marked by the suspension of the activities of all the vital organs, one may exist almost for any length of time without any physical degeneration or dissolution. This is what is called death here.

Our Bengal Vaishnava lyrics describe all these stages of insanity, coma and death in relation to Shree Radha, as stages of the development or evolution of her romantic passion for Shree Krishna. Though, generally speaking, these lyrics fall divided, as has been already said, into two classes, namely, the song of separation and the song of union, in reality they are all songs of separation. There is even during moments of the closest union a lurking fear of separation. There is a common saying that in union Shree Radha finds only one Shree Krishna, in separation the whole universe is full of Shree Krishna. Separation means the absence of the Lord from the realm of the outer senses. But He is never absent from the inner consciousness of the devotee. Outer sense-objects obstruct his beatific vision. But in his inner consciousness the universe is filled with the Divine Presence. In this state of complete *samadhi*, so closely corresponding to what we familiarly know as death, the devotee lives in the consciousness of the Divine Presence, and the familiar means of re-establishing the suspended relation between his inner self and outer world of his senses is to loudly sing the name of the Lord or repeat it into his ears. It is through the ear that the name of the Lord entering his inner consciousness leads to this *samadhi*, and it is through the ear again that the suspended relation between his inner consciousness and the outer world of senses is re-established. All these are clearly described in the lyrics of our Vaishnava poets.

The spiritual meaning and interpretation of these lyrics have been supplied by the direct realisations of the founder of Bengal Vaishnavism, Shree Chaitanya Mahaprabhu. Therefore, these *keertana*-s always start with a picture of the passion of Shree

Chaitanya Mahaprabhu. The ten stages of the evolution of the romance of our Vaishnavic *rasa*-s were produced or re-produced in the life of Shree Chaitanya. And though sometimes the Vaishnava poets have liberally drawn upon their own fancy, fed by the familiar Krishna legend, in painting the passion of Shree Chaitanya, the broad outlines of the romantic passion, evolving through the four outstanding stages of *purva-raga* or the longing previous to the actual union and enjoyment of the lover by his or her love, *milan*, or the first union, *mána* or repudiation of the lover by his love in a fit of jealousy, and *viraha* or separation,—marked also the realisations of Shree Chaitanya Mahaprabhu. And reference to these experiences of his furnish, therefore a real key to the meaning and interpretation of our Vaishnava *rasa-keertana*-s. It is easy to understand the lyrics depicting the romance of *purva-raga* or of the novice following his initiation Nor is it difficult to understand the romance of the first union. But it is exceedingly difficult to appreciate or even understand the romance of jealousy or *mána*. It is, however, an experience of the inner spiritual life. Whenever the devotee is possessed by the conceit of his love for the Lord, his heart dries up, and the consciousness of the Lord immediately fades from his mind and soul. The Lord forgives every other sin of his devotee, but He never forgives the sin of spiritual pride. This is really the meaning of the familiar Christian saying that the sin against the Father is forgiven, the sin against the Son is forgiven, but the sin against the Holy Ghost is never forgiven. The cloud of spiritual pride appearing in the smallest corner of our consciousness hardens our heart, and drives away the sense of the Divine Presence, leaving us in a state of utter desolation. This is the specific spiritual experience which our Vaishnava lyrics have essayed to sing as *mána* or jealousy. In a fit of this jealousy Shree Radha turns her face away from Shree Krishna. Shree Krishna tries to appease her by the many devices familiar to the worshipful lover. But He fails to remove her anger. Disappointed He leaves her. And then Shree Radha is brought to a consciousness of her own suicidal pride, and then starts a process of self-reproach and self-abasement. All these have been painted with exquisite skill and delicacy by the Vaishnava poets. And though these cannot, in all their detail, apply to the realisations of Shree Chaitanya Mahaprabhu, the reality of the spiritual experience following the sin of spiritual pride was so clearly manifest in the life of the Mahaprabhu that these Vaishnava lyrics furnish an exquisite and entrancing vehicle for the cultivation of the romance of Divine Love. This is how they have been used by successive generations of the Vaishnava devotees of Bengal for the last four hundred years and more. Read and interpreted through the actual realisations of Shree Chaitanya Mahaprabhu these Vaishnava lyrics will be found to furnish strong evidences of what may be called the individuality of the Bengalee people.

CHAPTER V.

Social Reconstruction and Mass Movement in Bengal Vaishnavism.

The Vaishnava Movement in Bengal, initiated by Shree Chaitanya Mahaprabhu, not only gave us a new theology of the Absolute or a new philosophy of art or created new forms of beauty through its lyrics,—the richest in the whole body of old Bengalee literature—but it delivered a new social message, the message of the presence of the Lord in every human individually and collectively in the human society, and applied itself to secure both individual and social uplift.

The Vaishnavic Movement all over India—that of Baba Nanak in the North-West or the Punjab, that of Kabir, Dadu and Ramananda in Upper India, of Tukaram in the Deccan, and of Shree Chaitanya Mahaprabhu in Bengal, of the 15th and 16th centuries—was the result of the contact of of ancient and mediaeval Hindu thought with the soul-compelling humanism of Islam as it was developed in its philosophy and poetry under the influence of the special culture of Persia. Islamic thought in coming into contact with the old Aryan thought of Persia, passed through transformations in its emotional and spiritual side somewhat similar to what happened to Christianity when it came in contact with Greek thought and culture. Had Islam come to India direct from Arabia, it could not have possibly found those affinities with the deeper thoughts and realisations of Hindu culture, that were absolutely essential to the success of its propaganda in this continent. Islamic piety and Islamic poetry of Persia made a strong appeal to the spiritual endeavours and realisations of mediaeval Hinduism, and called for a reconstruction of Hindu thought and life; these found more or less organised expression in and through this continental Vaishnavic upheaval among us. These Vaishnavic Movements, though they did not completely cut themselves off from the thoughts and realisations of ancient and mediaevel India, were really movements of protestagainst the current religion and social economy and institutions of the Hindu people. In the Punjab this continental Movement really gave birth to a new religion, Sikhism.

In the other Indian provinces this general *Bhakti* Movement all over India in the 15th and 16th centuries attempted a reconstruction of current Hindu thought and life with a view to make these an efficient vehicle of the new spiritual and social ideals. This was seen in a general movement of renaissance that became very marked in the domain of vernacular literature. Hindi in Upper India, Marathi in the Deccan, and Bengalee in our own province, received a new inspiration, becoming the vehicle of the new thought, creating a new body of religious and spiritual literature that had previously been practically confined to Sanskrit. These new creations at once helped to emancipate the genius of these various peoples from the domination of mediaeval Brahminism. In this way this general Vaishnava upheaval created a continental mass movement in India.

This mass movement was very powerful in Bengal, because of the antecedent cultural evolution of the Bengalee people with their inheritances in Buddhism. In the Punjab the religion of Baba Nanak created a new scripture of its own, that practically replaced the ancient scriptural authority of the Hindus. The Granth-Saheb became to the followers of Nanak, what the Vedas had from time immemorial been to the Hindus, the divine sanction for their religious culture and social economy. In Bengal the Movement of Shree Chaitanya did not or could not completely free itself from Brahminical domination. But without repudiating the authority of the divine revelation of the Vedas, practically Bengal Vaishnavism adopted Shree Chaitanya-Charitamrita, which embodied the life and teachings of Shree Chaitanya Mahaprabhu, as its special scripture. Shree Chaitanya-Charitamrita is practically a Bengalee book, though it has very copiously quoted the Bhagavata, the Bhagavad-Geeta, and even the Upanishads as ancient authority for and elucidation of the new thought and theology. Besides the Chaitanya-Charitamrita, Bengal Vaishnavism created other scriptures also, written exclusively or almost exclusively in the vernacular of the province. The Chaitanya-Mangal and Chaitanya-Bhagabata are both purely Bengalee compositions. And the Chaitanya-Charitamrita has itself very largely drawn upon these two original Bengalee books, and based its narration of the life and teachings of Shree Chaitanya Mahaprabhu upon these originals. These three books, the Chaitanya-Mangal, the Chaitanya-Bhagabata and the Chaitanya-Charitamrita, together constitute really the authoritative scripture of Bengal Vaishnavism. The result has been a great and wide mass movement among the Vaishnavas of Bengal. The devout Vaishnava has to read these books, as part of his daily devotions just as the Bible has to be read by the devout Christian, the Koran by the devout Moslem the Granth-Saheb by the devout Sikh, and the Upanishads and ancient Sanskrit scriptures, like the Bhagavad-Geeta and the Adhatma Ramayana, by the devout Hindu of the old school. The creation of religious scripture in the vernacular of the people gave at once a very powerful impetus to mass education in Bengal. The result of it was seen even in the early years of the present century, when the Vaishnavas of Bengal were found to be the only literates as a class among our Hindu population. Not only the males of this denomination but even their females became thus more or less educated in their own vernacular. Literacy, hitherto confined to the Brahmin from religious motives and to the so-called higher classes of non-Brahmins from secular motives, spread therefore among the very large large class of Bengalee Vaishnavas.

The Movement of Shree Chaitanya helped also very largely to emancipate the so-called lower classes or castes of Bengalee Hindus from the many social disabilities under which they had been living in the old Brahminical society. Shree Chaitanya Mahaprabhu tried to abolish the current caste exclusiveness of Brahminical Hinduism. He accepted many a qualified non-Brahmin, even of the so-called untouchable caste, food cooked or water touched by whom could not be taken by the so-called higher castes,—the Brahmins, the Kayasthas and the Vaidyas and their servitors,—into the ministry of his new congregation. These people became the *guru*-s or spiritual leaders or preceptors of the new community, taking equal place with the hereditary Brahmins, who joined the new Movement. They were all called Goswamis. These Vaishnava teachers received from their disciples the same reverence and social honour hitherto given only to the Brahmins. Not only this, but even Mahomedan saints like, for instance, Haridas, received the honour due to the

Brahmin; while Hindus, who had lost their caste through their intimate association with the Moslem court of the province, became, on their aceptance of the new code and culture of Vaishnavism, to be fully reinstated into their lost social and spiritual position in the new community, and became the acknowledged apostles and leaders of the thought and society of Shree Chaitanya's disciples, for instance, Rupa and Sanatana and their nephew Jeeva, who built up the new system of philosophy and aesthetics of our Vaishnavic cult. All these had a tremendous influence in working the uplift of the Bengalee masses, regardless of their birth, or social position in the old and orthodox Hindu community.

This new Vaishnavic Movement in Bengal tried, in fact, to create a new community, regulated not by the old social and sacerdotal laws that go under the general name of *Smriti*-s, but by a new social and sacramental code of their own. The result of this attempt was, however, not what the founder of Bengal Vaishnavism had clearly expected in compiling a new set of Vaishnavic laws. His object was to create a new and reformed community, freed from the trammels of the old and mediaeval Hindu society, particularly the bondage of Brahminical laws and customs. The laws of Shree Chaitanya Mahaprabhu attempted to revolutionise the current Brahminical law of marriage, which was dominated by the old and mediaevel laws of Hindu castes. According to the new Vaishnava law any Vaishnava might marry any other Vaishnava, of course outside the circle of consanguinity recognised by the old Hindu law, but without any regard for considerations of caste. A non-Brahmin, man or woman, might without offence marry a Brahmim woman or man. Not only Vaishnavas might inter-marry with one another, but they were also free from the mediaevel interdiction against adult marriage and widow-remarriage. The marriage ritual also was very much simplified, trying to go back to the *gandarbha* system of the old Hindu classification, regulated by personal attachment and selection of the parties, and not by the old caste-laws. The exchange of garlands or specifically of beads made of the stalks of the sacred *tulsi* plant, which was the denominational emblem or uniform of the Vaishnava sect, was considered enough to legalise these marriages.

As in the matter of marriage so also in the matter of *sradh* or after-death ceremony, the

Bengal Vaishnavas were emancipated from the trammels of ancient Vedic ritualism. The old magic was replaced by a simple ceremonial consisting of the singing of the name of the Lord and the feeding of brother Vaishnavas, which went by the general name of *mahotsava*.

The new Vaishnava community also abjured the worship of numerous gods and goddesses of the Hindu pantheon by setting up their images, replacing these ceremonials, steeped in the ancient spirit of Vedic magic and requiring therefore the services of the Brahmins, who were alone entitled to recite the Vedic texts and perform these rituals, by the singing of the name of the Lord and the feeding of Vaishnavas on every festive occasion. The general rule of religious life was summed-up by the familiar Bengalee couplet :

ना करिबे अन्य देवेर निन्दन वन्दन
ना करिबे अन्य देवेर प्रसाद भक्षण ।

"Thou shalt not abuse nor adore other gods (except the Lord Shree Krishna) nor shalt thou partake of the *prasada* or food offered to the other gods."

But converts to Shree Chaitanya's Vaishnava cult belonging to the higher castes of Hindus, the Brahmins, the Vaidyas and the

Kayasthas, could not sacrifice their social position to the demands of the new culture. All that they did was, therefore, only to adopt the so-called spiritual laws of it, namely, to accept their initiation at the hands of the Vaishnava *guru*-s, and pursue the spiritual and subjective disciplines of the new culture, while continuing to observe the general laws of Hindu society in regard to social and sacerdotal affairs. The new community of Vaishnavas in Bengal was thus divided almost from the very beginning into two sections, one consisting of those who were obedient to the laws of Chaitanya, and the other, though initiated in the worship of Shree Krishna, continuing in their loyalty to the old Brahminical laws. These two classes came to be known respectively as ***Chaitanya-anugata*** Vaishnavas and ***Smriti–anugata*** Vaishnavas. The latter were caste-Vaishnavas, and the former might be called outcaste-Vaishnavas. The caste-Vaishnavas maintained their position in the new Hindu commnnity as Brahmins or Vaidyas or Kayasthas and their servitors. The latter to whatever caste they might originally belong, were gradually condemned to a very low social position on account of their Bohemian ways, particularly in the matter of marriage.

On the other hand, gradually the Brahmins intrigued to secure a high position even in the new and reformed community. From the very beginning the Chaitanya Movement created a very large opening for the entrance of the old and mediaeval Brahminical hierarchy into its cult and culture by trying to filiate these to the Krishna legend. Shree Krishna worship had been associated with the worship of the symbol *Salagrama* or the so-called "Black Stone" representing the Narayana. This symbol became a common object of worship thus both to the new Vaishnavas and the old and orthodox Hindus, making a very easy bridge between the old Brahminism and the new Vaishnavism. Brahminical supremacy readily used this bridge to enter the new Vaishnava community, and assert its ancient domination over it, Shree Chaitanya Mahaprabhu's open attempt towards securing the emancipation of his cult and culture from the supernaturalism and ritualism of mediaeval Brahminical orthodoxy notwithstanding. The final result of the Brahminical intrigne in the new Vaishnava Movement was practically to repudiate the laws and sacraments of Shree Chaitanya as a heresy and condemn those who followed these practically to the position of Hindu outcastes, and instal the Brahminical *Smriti*-s as the authoritative laws and rituals of even the Hindus of the new Vaishnava denomination. But though the higher castes of the new Vaishnavas, the Vaidyas and the Kayasthas and their servitors, managed to keep themselves by this compromise within the fold of Hindu orthodoxy or respectability, the great bulk of the Vaishnavas, who naturally came from the lower castes, tried, so far as was possible under the circumstances, to keep up the new ideals.

This division of the new and reformed community into two sections, one within the fold of caste-ridden and Brahmin-dominated Hindu orthodoxy, and the other following the social code of Shree Chaitanya Mahaprabhu, and in consonance of it excommunicated from the orthodox Brahminical society, practically killed the spirit of the social message of the new Bengal school of Vaishnavism. The Vaishnavas also became consequently caste-ridden and except during their special denominational festivals failed to observe the high principles of the equality of man based upon the recognition of their fundamental divinity as manifestations of Narayana. Even the more pious among them, while trying to follow the ideal of Shree Chaitanya Mahaprabhu in their emotional culture, in practical social life and relations continued to be dominated by current Hindu customs under the *Varnashrama* law. As within the fold of Hindu orthodoxy there was a class of religious mendicants, who from their initiation into the order of the *sannyasin* repudiated all social distinctions and obligations, arising from their birth and heritage, even so there grew up a class of Vaishnava mendicants who followed the laws of Brahminical *sannyasa*. Among the Vaishnava mendicants also there grew up two sections, one which imitated the law of Shree Chaitanya himself, and other which imitated the law of life of the orthodox Hindu *sannyasin*.

These various social and socio-religious evolutions among the followers of Shree Chaitanya Mahaprabhu practically overwhelmed the ideal of humanism that had inspired his message. The cultivation of the love of God through the love and service of man and the realisation of God in every human being, which has been the very soul of Bengal Vaishnavism, was consequently lost in the revival of Brahminical supernaturalism, symbolism and caste-laws.

The superb humanism of the gospel of Shree Chaitanya Mahaprabhu and its message of the equality of man, built upon his fundamental divinity, was thus overwhelmed by the spirit of mediaeval Brahminism with its excessive emphasis on what may be called Subjective Idealism, and even the new Vaishnavic culture came to be dominated by an unreal and subjective emotionalism. Sentiment was divorced from sensibilities. The four *rasa*-s, namely, (i) the romance of the master and servitor relation, or the king and subject relation, or the parent and children relation, that went by the general name of *dasya*, (ii) the romance of friendship or *sakhya*, (iii) the romance of the filial affection or *batsalya*, and (iv) the soul-enthralling romance of the sex relation or *madhurya*—all these were divorced from the actual domestic and social relations upon which they are normally built. The Vaishnava devotees did not seek to realise these *rasa*-s by the idealisation and spiritualisation of their actual domestic and social life and relations, but by trying to imitate the old and mediaeval Krishna legend, and placing themselves subjectively in the position of the servitors, friends and parents of Shree Krishna; while as regards the last and the highest of these *rasa*-s, namely, that which proceeds from the romance of the man and woman relation, the Vaishnava devotees sought to vicariously realise it by fancying themselves to be the *sakhee*-s or boon companions of Shree Radha. In this way, the realistic emphasis of the *bhakti* cult of Bengal was completely removed, and substituted by a system of fanciful and subjective emotionalism. Shree Chaitanya's Movement had entered a strong protest against the Samkara-Vedanta doctrine of *Maya* or Illusion as the origin of the world-process. That was responsible for the monkish monasticism of our mediaeval Hinduism. This return to mediaeval subjectivism and fancies of the old spiritual life and culture helped very materially to revive the doctrine of *Maya* or Illusion even among the Vaishnavas themselves. The world was *mayik*, illusory; all the relations of life came to be regarded as a delusion and a snare by the followers of Shree Chaitanya Mahaprabhu himself, so that there was little or nothing to choose between mediaeval Brahminism and the cult and culture that passed as Vaishnavism.

But the most distinctive note of the Movement of Shree Chaitanya Mahaprabhu was its universalism. It repudiated the mediaeval Hindu dogma of *adhikaree-veda* or the classification of worships according to the qualification of the worshipper. This dogma had been organised in the mediaeval institution of caste. The Brahmins, being regarded as the best qualified, claimed by virtue of their birth the right of the highest and purest Divine worship. Shree Chaitanya Mahaprabhu repudiated this dogma of *adhikaree-veda.* The highest and purest worship of the Lord consisted in the repetition of His Holy Name. This required no rituals, no offerings of flowers or leaves or edibles to the Deity, or the services of the Brahmins. Every devotee could perform this worship himself. Whoever took the name of the Lord became purified in both mind and body by that one single act, and was qualified to worship the Lord. In this way the Bengal Vaishnava cult completely repudiated the mediaeval Hindu dogma of *adhikaree-veda*, and thus granted the highest religious franchise, hitherto enjoyed by the Brahmins only, to all men and women, irrespective of all considerations of birth, parentage and social status. It proclaimed the

9

great gospel of universal worship by declaring

> हरेर्नाम, हरेर्नाम, हरेर्नामैव केवलम्
> कलौ नास्त्येव नास्त्येव नास्त्येव गतिरन्यथा ।

The name of the Lord, the name of the Lord, the name of the Lord is the only way (to salvation); there is no other way, no other way, no other way, in this age.

And the Mahaprabhu added to this injunction another indicating the mental, moral and social discipline that must accompany the worship of the Lord through repeating His name :

> तृणादपि सुनीचेन तरोरिव सहिष्णुना
> अमानिना मानदेन कीर्त्तनीयः सदा हरिः ।

This must not be a mere mechanical function. The name of the Lord must be uttered and recited in a spirit of utmost humility. This is the first condition of the true Vaishnavic worship ; the second condition is that it must be uttered in a spirit of long suffering or devoid of any ill-will towards even one's worst enemies ; and, third, giving honour to others without seeking any honour for one's own self. The literal meaning of the couplet is : "Humbler than the humblest blade of grass (that does not refuse to be trampled upon by any one), long suffering as the tree (that does not refuse to return good for evil, and never withdraws its shade even from those that go to cut it), seeking no honour for one's own self but always giving honour to others,–in this spirit must the name of the Lord be chanted."

This remarkable couplet really sums up the entire philosophy and ethics of the cult and culture of Bengal Vaishnavism. The pursuit of this discipline involves the realisation of the Lord in every human being. The spirit of humility enjoined here is not a mere ethical quality. It is not that self-depreciation which usually passes for humility. It is rather that complete unconsciousness of self which follows the consciousness of the Divine Presence. The long suffering, spoken of here, is also the direct result of Universal God-consciousness. This universal God-consciousness is the key to the Vaishnavic worship of the Lord through the repetition of His name. It is both the way and the end of this worship. This simple formula and ritual, if ritual it can at all be called, of the worship of the Lord as enjoined by Bengal Vaishnavism, made the Movement of Shree Chaitanya

Mahaprabhu a large missionary movement in Hinduism. Non-Hindus had been Hinduised before also, but it was done by the imposition of the Hindu social economy or the caste-and-order system upon the non-Hindus. It was in this way that the Huns and the Sakas and other peoples that had migrated to India from beyond our North-Western frontier were able to be assimilated into the Hindu society of this continent. But the Movement of Shree Chaitanya Mahaprabhu repudiated the caste-and-order law or *varnashrama-dharma* of mediaeval Hinduism, relegating it to a lower stage of religious and social evolution. The Mahaprabhu introduced a new and universal method of proselytisation. While the other missionary religions like, for instance, Christianity or Islam or even the older Buddhistic system tried to bring strangers into their fold through the propagation of their special creeds, and whoever accepted their creed were admitted into their fraternity, regardless of their race, colour, country or other accidents of birth and heritage, Shree Chaitanya Mahaprabhu inculcated no creed at all but simply administered the initiation of the simple name of the Lord to the neophytes, and enjoined the very simple rule of life enunciated in the well-known Bengalee couplet, interdicting the adoration or the abuse of other objects of worship except the Lord Shree Krishna, and the partaking of the *prasada* of or offerings made to any other deity. This missionary method prevented the Mahaprabhu's Vaishnavic propaganda from assuming a militant character. There was no room in it for what is known in Christian literature as "the Church Militant", much less had it any manner of apology for the religious rivalries and antagonisms familiar to the Islamic culture. Inside the Hindu communion, the message of Shree Chaitanya Mahaprabhu emancipated the lower castes from their age-long trammels, admitting them on terms of equality with the so-called higher castes in all Vaishanvic congregations. It inculcated the ideal :

चण्डालोऽपि द्विजश्रेष्ठ हरिभक्तिपरायणः ।

Even the Chandaler who is devoted to Shree Hari, is superior to the Brahmin ; the Brahmin devoid of the love of Hari is lower than the Chandala. This Vaishnavic ideal worked a silent revolution in the caste-ridden Brahminical social order. Outside the Hindu communion, the Mahaprabhu's message proselytised entire non-Hindu clans by initiating them in the name of the Lord, and offering them the very simple rule of domestic and social life promulgated by him. We thus find the whole clan of the Manipuris in north-eastern India becoming Vaishnavas of the school of Shree Chaitanya Mahaprabhu.

CHAPTER VI.

The Promise of Bengal Vaishnavism and Its Fulfilment.

The cult and culture initiated by Shree Chaitanya Mahaprabhu worked for a reconciliation between the sensuous and the super-sensuous or the spiritual, between man's sense activities and his spiritual intuitions, between the realities of life and the idealities of religion. Though every religion had aimed to reach this result, few or none had been able to achieve it. Philosophic abstractions and monkish repressions had dominated the religious and spiritual endeavours practically of every religion, specially after it had passed what may be called the earliest naturalistic stage of its evolution.

In the earliest stage man had not created a gulf between the sensuous and the super-sensuous. The consciousness of the unseen, as distinct from if not opposed to the seen, had not as yet dawned upon the human mind. In this stage man universally found his God in the nature-objects about him. All the Vedic deities belong more or less to this class.

Agni, Indra, Varuna, the Maruts, the heavenly twins—Asvini Kumaras, Savita or the sun—all these names of the Vedic gods refer to the sense-experiences of the Vedic man. As in the Aryan cultures so also in the origin of Semitic religions the same thing is found. The Hebrew conception of the Godhead as El-Elohim or Lord Almighty is also derived from man's experiences of the forces of Nature.

Gradually, however, with the expansion of knowledge of natural objects and phenomena, this simple faith was disturbed by persistent questionings of man's awakened thought; ultimately it was destroyed by the logic of this thought. A great and impassable gulf was thus created between the sensuous and the super-sensuous, between man's perception of material objects and his intuition of the super-sensuous or the spiritual. In this stage man sought his God in the abstractions of his thought, and practically relegated the Ultimate Reality to the realm of the Unknown and the Unknowable. This, instead of helping, on the contrary, almost infinitely widened the gulf between the seen and the unseen, or between the sensuous and the super-sensuous or the spiritual, and started a course of religious and spiritual endeavours marked by logical abstractions and poetic fancies.

These two are the universal characteristics of what is called mediaeval thought. All the great world religions have been dominated by these almost upto the present day. Mediaeval religion everywhere made the obviously impossible attempt to raise man above the realities of his actual life and experience. The bogey of anthropomorphism possessed them all. Yet man found it impossible to conceive his God except in the terms of himself and his social relations and experiences. From the earliest times in every religion, or almost every religion, man has addressed his Maker as his Father, or as his King or Lord or Master, or as his Friend and Protector. And in all this he has applied to his God his direct personal realisations of his domestic and social life. The truth and reality of these various appellations of God are found in man's direct social experiences. When man addressed his God as "God Almighty", which is the familiar epithet in all Semitic religions, he tried to realise His presence and power in the forces of Nature about him. When he addressed his God as King and Protector he similarly tried to realise His presence and power in the social government to which he was subject. When he addressed Him as Father or Friend, he tried similarly to realise Him in his direct personal experience of his relations with his own father or friend and more intimately in his own realisations of fatherhood or friendship. Man thus at every stage of his religious and spiritual evolution, or of the progress of his personal God-consciousness, has tried to realise his Deity in and through his own inner and outer life and experience. Man's religion has always been, therefore, anthropomorphic. It was only in what may be called the mediaeval stage of his religious life, dominated by the conflict between the sensuous and the super-sensuous and the seen and the unseen, between the Creator and the created, that man was possessed by this fear of thinking of his God in the terms of his own life and experience.

This fear ignored the obvious fact that man cannot possibly know, love or serve except in the light of the reality of his own thought and experiences. All knowledge is really self-knowledge; all love is really self-love, though not in the vulgar sense of selfishness; and all service is really self-service. In plain English, this means that there are in our composition two elements, one ideal, and the other real.

The real is constantly seeking to approach the ideal. The ideal is constantly seeking to seize and draw the real towards itself. These two elements of our composite nature cannot be separated one from the other. They co-exist like what our ancients called shine and shadow. The universal and the particular thus exist together. The universal is implicit in every particular, and the particular seeks always to make the universal, which is implicit in it, explicit. Man and God thus exist together. One cannot be separated from the other. Any attempt to do so must destroy the reality of both. Yet the two cannot be identified with one another either without similarly destroying the reality and truth of both. This is the central God-idea as it is also the central man-idea in the philosophy of Bengal Vaishnavism.

To realise this mystery of God and man, we must first and foremost of all conquer our carnal desires and appetites, conquer them but not repress or try to destroy our natural appetites. This can only be achieved by the idealisation or spiritualisation of our normal and natural instincts and passions. Even without being conscious of their God reference we experience this idealisation and spiritualisation in those rare moments when our carnal passions rise to the plane of the truly romantic and our love loses itself into the Infinite. It is, however, a very rare experience. Ordinarily, our passions and appetites, born of our sense-contacts, remain imprisoned within the limits of the sensuous. Therefore, the realisation of the high Vaishnavic truths is exceedingly rare even among professed Vaishnavas, who either lose themselves in gross sensual enjoyments or seek their ideal in the abstractions and fancies of mediaeval theology and religion, using only the Vaishnavic terminologies and setting up fanciful Vaishnavic symbols.

The message of Shree Chaitanya Mahaprabhu failed, therefore, to be correctly understood or followed by the Vaishnava crowd who, partly by their ignorance and largely by their emotional fancies, destroyed all the fundamental notes of the cult and culture of the Mahaprabhu. They did even worse in their attempt to reconcile the message of the Mahaprabhu with current Hindu cult and culture, dominated by the abstractions of Samkara-Vedantic monism in its worst form, as found in the interpretations of the Panchadashee school. Even Vaishnavic exegetics and apologetics openly tried to explain away the obvious meaning of some of the fundamental doctrines of the Chaitanya school. The result of it has been that there is to-day hardly anything except mere words and symbols and the externals of sectarian cult and culture to distinguish between the gospel of Shree Chaitanya Mahaprabhu and popular mediaeval Brahminism.

Shree Chaitanya Mahaprabhu had declared in his life-time that there were only three and a half Vaishnavas in the world. But since his ascension his following has increased and can be counted in tens of millions Not one perhaps among them clearly understands the deep spirituality of the cult and culture inaugurated by him. The spirit of Hindu mediaevalism hadcompletely overwhelmed the realism of the Chaitanya cult. Yet the modern man cried for the things for which Shree Chaitanya's Movement stood. A revival of the true message of Bengal Vaishnavism was called for. This revival came, though unconsciously, through the Movement of modern religion and society, initiated in Bengal by Raja Ram Mohan Roy.

Raja Ram Mohan, however, had little knowledge and less appreciation of the underlying rationalism and spirituality of the cult and culture of Bengal Vaishnavism. He had a strong prejudice against the teachings and traditions of the *Goswami*-s or the Vaishnava teachers of Bengal. Considering the evil ways into which popular Vaishnavism had fallen in Bengal, this was not at all strange. The Raja's personal religion and piety were built partly upon the theosophy of our ancient Upanishads, and partly upon Islamic rationalism and the refined romance of Islamic poetry. Though his theology recognised and proclaimed the essential unity of God and man, Raja Ram Mohan was evidently scared away from the highest Vaishnavic realisations by the bogey of identifying man with God. For one thing, this was a stumbling block on his way to the acceptance of the fundamental doctrines of Bengal Vaishnavism; for another, the gross sensualism of the familiar Vaishnavic *bhakti* culture through the four *rasa*-s evidently turned the Raja's bowels against it. But the Samkara-Vedantic monism, or even the modified form of it adopted by his Brahmo Samaj, could not meet the demands of the spiritual and emotional life of his people. The Brahmo Samaj cried out for a *bhakti* cult that would rationally filiate itself with the new Brahmo theology. Personally both Raja Ram

Mohan and Maharshi Devendra Nath, who succeeded him in the leadership of the new Movement, drew the materials for the building up of their emotional life from Islam. But the great bulk of the adherents of the new Movement were not familiar with Persian poetry and the literature of *bhakti* in Islam. They could not, therefore, follow Raja Ram Mohan or Maharshi Devendra Nath in the pursuit of the emotional side of their religious and spiritual culture. Keshub Chunder Sen at first drew his inspiration of *bhakti* or love of God from the literature of Christianity. But this source was not also as open to the general body of the members of the new Movement as it was to Keshub and his lieutenant Pratap Chandra Mazoomdar and a few others of Keshub's missionary group. This want of the great bulk of the members of the Brahmo Samaj was met by Bijoy Krishna Goswami, who helped Keshub to inaugurate a new *bhakti* movement in the Brahmo Samaj, more or less filiated to the Movement of Shree Chaitanya Mahaprabhu.

Shree Chaitanya's Movement failed to achieve its object, because it was not, so far as the crowd was concerned, built upon the highest realisations of the Upanishads and the Vedanta. Universal God-vision is the culmination of Vedantic culture. He who has attained this high illumination, realises Brahman in every object, animate and inanimate. To him every human is a concrete revelation or manifestation of Brahman. To him there is no such thing as mere man. Man is essentially a spiritual being, not only viewed in the abstract, separated from his physical or physiological organisation, but in the completeness of his individuality or personality, composed both of his body and his soul. This realisation produces that absolute equanimity which is called the *shanta bhava* in the literature of Bengal Vaishnavism. This *shanta bhava* is an absolute condition-precedent of the cultivation and realisation of that *bhakti* which is called *raganuga* in Vaishnavic literature.

The spiritual illumination generally called *Brahma-jnanam* or the realisation of Brahman in all objects, human and non-human, was the ostensible aim and objective of the theology and disciplines of the new Brahmo Samaj. This was, however, actually achieved by few. The multitude, who abjured current Hindu ritualism and symbolism and tried to follow the new social ideal of the Samaj that repudiated all caste-restrictions and strove for a freer domestic and social life, more or less in conformity with the modern European gospel of Equality, Fraternity and Humanity, failed to understand the deep spiritual implications of their own dogmas, with the result that they were not able to acquire that absolute equanimity based upon universal God-consciousness, which alone could possibly fulfil the mission of the Movement of Shree Chaitanya Mahaprabhu. The need of a Vaishnavic revival in Bengal thus remained unaffected by the Movement of the new Brahmo Samaj.

The neo-Vaishnavic Movement, which followed in the wake of the social reaction and so-called religious revival that came with the decline of the influence of the Brahmo protest, during the closing years of the last century, also miserably failed to meet the demands of the mission of Shree Chaitanya Mahaprabhu. This Movement was practically a Movement of religious reaction, that tried to revive the ideals and disciplines of mediaeval Brahminism that had overwhelmed the rationalistic and humanistic gospel of Shree Chaitanya Mahaprabhu. This neo-Vaishnavism was itself obsessed by the supernaturalism and symbolism of mediaeval Brahminical *bhakti* cult and culture. Its only distinctive feature was its social message which tried to remove the ban that the Brahminical caste-system had placed upon certain so-called lower sections of the Hindu community. The apotheosis of man, which was the central doctrine of the Chaitanya Movement, was not appreciated by this neo-Vaishnavism. Shree Krishna, therefore, remained even to the new Vaishnavas *a god* among the many gods of the Hindu pantheon. Shree Krishna was worshipped as an incarnation or *avatara*, but not really as *avataree* or the Ultimate Reality from whom all *avatara*-s emanated.

Radha Krishna were not gods; Radha Krishna were not smybolic representations of the mystery of the Godhead. Shree Krishna was not the Supreme Soul, and Shree Radha was not symbolic of the human soul. This was the fundamental dogma of the Radha-Krishna cult in the thought and realisation of Shree Chaitanya Mahaprabhu's Vaishnavism. Radha-Krishna was to this realisation the Ultimate Reality or *Parama-Tattva*. What the Upanishads call Brahman is only an effulgence of the reality of Shree Krishna; what the *yogee*-s worship as *Paramatma* or the Indweller, the Eternal Witness in individual life and consciousness as well as in the collective life and consciousness of humanity,—is only a partial aspect of the Ultimate Reality which is Shree Krishna. This Shree Krishna is not an abstraction. He is not a mere logic of thought. He is neither without-body, nor has He physical bodies like our own. He is eternally self-revealed in His own Being as well as progressively self-revealing through processes of cosmic and human evolution. He is the logic of all our sense-knowledge. He is the logic of all our self-realisations, physical, mental, moral or social, as well as spiritual. He is the Superman, Who is the key to all our ethical and aesthetic realisations and judgments, the Objective of all social and ethical as well as personal endeavours towards perfection. In Him are all revelations. From Him is all creation. From Him has come all religious Dispensations and towards Him move all religious and socio-religious codes, and in Him they find their final objective and self-fulfilment. This Shree Krisnha is the Universal Man towards Whom all humanity, both individually and collectively, are moving. He is the Universal Organism and all the nations and races of the world are His limbs and organs. The gospel of Shree Krishna as delivered by Shree Chaitanya Mahaprabhu is thus the gospel of Universal Humanity, that knows no distinction between Brahmin and Chandala or between Aryan and non-Aryan or between Hindu and non-Hindu. In Him are all races one ; all religions one ; all cults and cultures one, that lead under different names and through different forms and formu laries ultimately to the perfection of our common humunity.

APPENDIX

The Doctrine of Incarnation according to the Bengal School of Vaishnavism.

This article was written by Mr. Pal to form part of a chapter of the life-sketch of Nityananda by the late Bulloram Mullick and was published in his "Hindu Review" (1913).

The Doctrine of Incarnation according to the Bengal School of Vaishnavism.

The idea of incarnation is innate in the very structure of the theological speculations of the Hindus. This theology is fundamentally monistic. The Ultimate Reality is One, not two or many. It is One-without-a-Second. "Before all this was, my beloved, the Real alone existed," we read in the Upanishads. That Reality desired to be many for the object of creation, and He became many. This is Hindu cosmogony. This world-process is the process, really, of the One becoming many. The entire series of cosmic evolution is, thus, a perpetual process of incarnation or descent as it is really called in Sanskrit. But besides this general view there are also special views of Divine Incarnation in Hinduism. All creation is an incarnation of the Ultimate Reality. But He is not equally manifest in all created things. In the Bhagavad-Geeta we are, therefore, told that He is the highest and the best of every class. This is what may perhaps be called the cosmic view of the doctrine of Incarnation.

There is, however, a yet higher view of this doctrine in Hinduism. It may be called the historic view. This historic view is really the highest Geeta doctrine of Incarnation. We read in the Geeta:

> यदा यदा हि धर्मस्य ग्लानिर्भवति भारत।
> अभ्युत्थानमधर्मस्य तदात्मानम् सृजाम्यहम् ॥
> परित्राणाय साधुनाम् विनाशाय च दुष्कृताम्।
> धर्मसंस्थापनार्थाय सम्भवामि युगे युगे ॥

It means that God incarnates Himself whenever *dharma* or the moral sense of mankind becomes diseased and when *adharma* or that which is opposed to *dharma* rises to overwhelm society. The object of all incarnation is to save goodness, destroy evil and establish a true sense of duty on earth. Those who render our *dharma* into religion in English, take a narrow view of the former concept. In fact, on the human plane *dharma* connotes Duty in its largest sense, and includes duty to self, duty to one's family, duty to Society and the State, and duty to God and the world at large. And when we take *dharma* in this sense, the Geeta theory of Incarnation cannot be disputed. Every Great-Man, as Carlyle calls them, or every

Representative Man, to use the terminology of Emerson, every *mahapurusha*,—Buddha, Jesus, Mahommed, Sree Chaitanya Mahaprabhu,—was born at critical epochs of the history of their race and country, and worked to uphold the good, overthrow the evil and establish the supremacy of the moral and the spiritual life among men. Every one of them was, therefore, an *avatara* or Incarnation, according to the view of the Bhagavad-Geeta. This word *avatara* literally means not incarnation but only descent, though in this act of descent, the spirit has to take form in the flesh. Nor should this descent be understood as a physical act, namely, from heaven to earth. It is "descent" in the moral and spiritual sense. It means that the Unknown and the Unknowable becomes known and knowable. Transcendentalism postulates and posits a formless and attributeless Deity, if Deity it may at all be called. And God's *avatara* or descent would be meaningless and would serve absolutely no purpose, if it did not mean that in thus manifesting Himself to mankind He, who is really without name and form and all attributes and activities, did *assume* a Form and *all* excellent qualities or attributes.

Starting from the above premisses, one has

to determine for one's self, whether the *avatara* of Navadvipa was a historical reality. The Bengal school of Vaishnavism has accepted and proclaimed Shree Chaitanya Mahaprabhu as an *avatara*, the latest and the highest *avatara* of Shree Krishna. There are many Hindus who are not Vaishnavas, yet who do not feel called upon to contest this claim. There are others of a strongly sceptical turn of mind, who have in the past, even as in our own day, strongly repudiated these pretensions. It has, indeed, always been so. Buddha, Jesus, Mahammed, all the *avatara*-s, and prophets of the world, have been so treated by their opponents and by the faithless in every country and in every age. Jesus was regarded as a huge impostor by the teachers of Judaism. Shree Chaitanya Mahaprabhu was similarly looked upon by the teachers of the popular and corrupt Brahminism of his time in Bengal. The Jews repudiated the message of Jesus. The Brahmins of Navadvipa, the *etite* of that Hindu University, would not accept Shree Chaitanya Mahaprabhu. Jesus's message had, therefore, to be delivered to the Gentiles, through whom it was communicated to the world. Shree Chaitanya Mahaprabhu's message also had to be similarly delivered, mainly, to the unsophisticated non-Brahmin classes, and through them it was communicated to society at large. There is, thus, a kind of parallelism between the messages of these two *Mahapurushas* that strikes the mind of even the most superficial student of these two religious movements. The outer social effect of these two messages were also very similar. The Gentiles were comforted in spirit by accepting Jesus and his gospel of salvation. So were the non-Brahmin communities of Bengal comforted by accepting Shree Chaitanya Mahaprabhu and his message of love. The Gentiles were filled with a new hope, so were the non-Brahminical classes. God was not the monopoly of the Jewish Rabbis, thought now the Gentiles. God was not the monopoly of the Hindu Brahmins, felt and found now the non-Brahmins. To the Gentiles the Mosaic Law was nothing, the faith that Jesus gave was everything. To the non-Brahmins, the Brahminical rituals were really nothing; they had neither part nor lot in the Brahminical worships; they were, at best, mere worshippers at the gate. The name of the Lord that Shree Chaitanya Mahaprabhu gave them became everything. They could not study the Vedas. They could not recite the *mantra*-s. They neither understood nor were taught, nor indeed allowed to read and understand, these sacred texts and laws. Religious ritual was to them practically mere magic and incantation. But Shree Chaitanya Mahaprabhu gave to each man the right and the power to directly worship the Supreme Lord by chanting and singing His name. The old *puja*-s and *yajna*-s were nothing really to the people at large. The *Harinama* that they received from the Mahaprabhu became something personal and intimate to them, became, indeed, everything in their religious and spiritual life. The gospel of Jesus was preached far and wide; so has been the gospel of Shree Chaitanya amid the wildest popular enthusiasm.

But the real spiritual message, whether of Jesus or of Shree Chaitanya had at first no vital relation to the question whether they were or were not true *avatara*-s or incarnations of God. The question did not at all arise during the life-time of Jesus. Even the Messianic idea, which was a distinctly Jewish idea, though perhaps believed in during Jesus's life-time by some of his immediate adherents, did not receive much serious attention until after his death. It cannot be said that the question whether Shree Chaitanya Mahaprabhu was or was not an *avatara* did not at all arise during his life. If contemporary records are to be believed, it seems absolutely certain that all the most prominent associates and disciples of Shree Chaitanya Mahaprabhu did accept him as such. It was also very easy and natural for them to do so. The *avatara* idea is inherent in the Hindu consciousness. There had never before been any previous incarnation of God in the Jewish or even in the Greeko-Roman tradition. In Hinduism there had been many *avatara*-s before Shree Chaitanya Mahaprabhu. Not to mention the series beginning with Matsya or Fish and ending with Nri-Simha or Man-Lion, which represents what may perhaps be called the cosmic process of the evolution of God-man or God-in-man, there were even many incarnations on the purely human and historic plane, such as Shree Krishna, Shree Rama-Chandra, Bamana, Parashu rama and Buddha. The idea is thus familiar to the Hindu mind. It has percolated to the lowest strata of Hindu thought and imagination through the Puranas; and it is still further propagated and explained through a thousand *katha*-s and *yatra*-s or passion-plays. The Hindu mind is, thus, steeped in these ideas. It is a universally-accepted doctrine that whenever there is decay of *dharma* and the rise of *adarma*, the Lord Shree Krishna causes Himself to be born on earth for the upholding of goodness, the overthrow of evil and the establishment of *dharma* suited to the special requirements of the time. Consequently when Shree Chaitanya started upon his mission in Navadvipa, the Vaishnavas of the place, who in the agony of their soul had for years been calling upon Shree Krishna to come down and save his people and uplift the world, found no difficulty in accepting him as an *avatara*.

But though Shree Chaitanya Mahaprabhu was accepted and privately proclaimed among themselves as an *avatara* by his personal friends and immediate disciples even in his life-time, it was only after his death really that the idea was fully developed in the literature and philosophy of Bengal Vaishnavism. Like almost every theological school of the old times, the Vaishnava Hindus also base their speculations mainly upon ancient scriptures. In the first place, like the other Hindu schools, the Vaishnavas also appeal to the Upanishads as their *revealed* authority.

And one of the principal texts which they cite in support of their special philosophy of life is that wherein the Ultimate Reality is described as *anandam* or Joy or Bliss. There can be no joy, unless there is present before an enjoyer an adequate object of his enjoyment. And the psychology of *anandam* or joy is always this, namely, that in every act or experience of joy or *anandam*, the enjoyer goes out of himself, so to say, to the object of his enjoyment, and taking it up comes back to himself. As in every act of knowledge, to quote the dictum of Hegel, the self goes out of itself to return to itself to be itself so in every act of enjoyment also the enjoyer goes out of himself to the object of his enjoyment and unites it with himself, and thus comes back to himself to be himself or to fulfil himself. The process means thus, an act of self-differentiation, followed by an act of re-integraion. Homogeniety has to be broken up by Duality and the Duality to be completed in Unity. The Ultimate Reality is thus in the beginning, if we may use a term in the time series in regard to that which is beyond and above that series, Homogenous. It is Undifferentiated Being. It is Pure Being. It is *nirgunam*. It is Transcendental; Unknown and Unknowable. But It differentiates Itself from Itself, and the two self-differentiated Selves become *Purusha* and *Prakriti*. *Purusha* is the Subject, the Knower. *Prakriti* is the Object or the Known. *Purusha* is the Enjoyer, *Prakriti* is the Object of the *Purusha's* enjoyment. All knowledge or thought or consciousness, as well as all joy and bliss, is in the union of *Purusha* and *Prakriti*. The object is meaningless without its subject, a mere nothing. The enjoyed is meaningless without its enjoyer. The object of a self-conscious subject cannot be itself unconscious; for then, the subject cannot possibly realise himself fully through it. Every consciousness knows itself fully only by standing face to face with its own counterpart, with an object that thought different from it is yet entirely like itself. We know ourselves not by knowing material objects so much, if at all, as we do by making other humans like ourselves the object of our thought. So also our highest enjoyments come only from our own kind, from other self-conscious beings, who though objects of our enjoyments, are yet themselves also enjoyers like ourselves, and can therefore reciprocate our emotions more or less. In the

Mystery of the Divine Being there is, therefore, a similar Duality; and these two mutually supplement each other, are mutually necessary for each other, and help each other, not only in their mutual self-realisation, but equally also in the self-realisation of the Whole of which these are self-differentiated aspects. This, very briefly, is the philosophy of Vaishnavic Dualism. It is a Dualism that fulfils but does not destroy the essential Unity of the Ultimate Reality. *Purusha* and *Prakriti* are not two entities but really One Being—One is *ousia* or essence, different in *hypostates* or appearance, as the Christian theologians would say. *Purusha* is Shree Krishna. *Prakriti* is Shree Radha. They are two persons, but one Being. Person is from Latin *persona* a mask. Their difference or duality is the result of a mask that each puts on for purposes of sport or *leela*, as the Vaishnavas would say. This is, in brief, the fundamental philosophy of the Ultimate Reality or *Parama-Tattva* of the Bhagavata. The Bengal school of Vaishnavism takes its stand upon this philosophy.

In the Bhagavata (Part I, Chapter I, 11th, *sloka*) we read :—

वदन्ति तत्तत्त्वविदस्तत्त्वं यज्ज्ञानमद्वयं ।
ब्रह्मेति परमात्मेति भगवानिति शब्द्यते ॥
11

Those who know the *Tattva* call that One-undivided-Consciousness as *Tattva,* which goes by the name of Brahman (in the Upanishads), Paramatman or the Indweller or Over-Soul (among the *yogee*-s), and Bhagavan (by the schools of Love and Faith). The Vaishnavas say that this Bhagavan is Shree Krishna Himself and none other. Bhagavan is the Perfect Person. He is the Supreme *Purusha.* He is the abode of All-Power, All-Knowledge, All-Penance, All-*Yoga,* All-Bliss and All-Beauty. Brahman of the Upanishads is only an aspect, a moment, a mere effulgence of the body of Bhagavan. The Paramatma or the Indweller of the *yogee*-s is also a mere aspect of His. Bhagavan is the Full, the Complete, the Perfect Person, the Supreme and Absolute Reality.

Following this Bhagavata doctrine of what may perhaps be called the true Hindu Trinity, the followers of Shree Chaitanya Mahaprabhu declare :—

यदद्वैतं ब्रह्मोपनिषदि तदप्यस्य तनुभा ।
य आत्मान्तर्यामीपुरुष इति सोऽस्यांशविभवः ॥
षड़ैश्वर्यैःपूर्णो य इह भगवान् स स्वयमयं ।
न चैतन्यात् कृष्णाज्जगति परतत्त्वं परमिह ॥

That which is the One-and-undifferentiated

Brahman in the Upanishads is the effulgence of the body of this (Shree Krishna-Chaitanya). He who is called the Person-residing-in-the soul, is the mere part-manifestation of this (Shree Krishna Chaitanya). He who is full with the six-fold powers and qualities, and is called here (in the Bhagavata) Bhagavan, He is Himself this (Shree Krishna-Chaitanya). There is no *Tattva* or Reality in this world, superior to Shree Krishna Chaitanya.

It will thus be seen that the followers of Shree Chaitanya Mahaprabhu absolutely identify him with Shree Krishna and thus they not only make him an *Avatara* but actually take him above the incarnation series. For Shree Krishna is not, they say. an *Avatara* or incarnation, but is the Supreme Being Himself—the *Avataree* or He who is incarnated.

But the doctrine of incarnation as propounded by the Bengal school of Vaishnavism goes much further, and, one might even add, much deeper than the Geeta doctrine. To revive decadent *dharma*, to put down the ascendent *adharma*, to save the good, to overthrow evil-doers, and to establish the highest and the best social order suited to the genius and requirements of a particular age,—these are the objects of the *avatara* or descent of Shree Krishna or the Supreme Lord. This is the Geeta doctrine. This is true; say the Bengal Vaishnavas. But it is not the whole truth. *Avatara*-s or incarnations are of various classes. Some are incarnations of particular powers of the Lord. Brahma is, thus, the incarnation of His Creative Power; Vishnu is, similarly, the incarnation of the Protective Power of Shree Krishna. To revive decadent *dharma*, to save the righteous, to punish evil-doers, to establish Law and Order, to put down anarchy,—all these are really protective functions. For these, it is not at all necessary that Shree Krishna Himself should descend on earth at a special time and at a particular place. These are all functions of Vishnu. But Shree Krishna descended on earth for His own inner reason. That object was realised, not in the overthrow of Kamsa or the destruction of Shishupala, nor in or by anything that Shree Krishna did at Kurukshetra, as the Charioteer of Arjuna, but in His life at Shree Brindabana, in and through His relations of love and affection with Nanda and Jashoda, who looked upon Him as their child, with Balaram, Sreedam, Sudam and the other youthful cowherds, who looked upon him as their friend and playmate, and with the Braja-Gopinees or the damsels of the cowherds of Braja-dhama who looked upon him as their lover. In Dvaraka, as a Prince of the Yadavas; in the court and camp of the Pandavas,—where He played the part of statesman and warrior, planned and executed the overthrow of Duryodhana and others for the establishment of a Kingdom of Righteousness or a *Dharma-Rajya*, there was only a partial revelation of the Lord. Here He was only the Protector of the world. It was only His Vishnu-aspect that was manifested here. But the real *Avatara*, the full and perfect revelation, was in Shree Brindabana. This Brindabana-*Leela* was the Supreme Object of the descent of Shree Krishna in the Dvapara-*Yuga*. It was a revelation of the innermost life and being of Shree Bhagavan or the Supreme Person. Here in Shree Brindabana He sported as in His Own Being, with His Own *Prakriti*. Though manifested here below, the thing itself was really super-mundane. It was a manifestation not of Shree Krishna's powers, but of Himself and His Love. Here He stood not as King or Saviour, not as the Lord of the Universe and the Author of all beings; but only as son, and friend, and lover. Here in Brindabana He sported in these sweet and tender and intimate relations, loving and being loved by Nanda and Jashoda, who tended Him as their child; by the youthful cowherds who played and romped with Him as their dearly-beloved mate; and by the damsels of Brindabana, who placed their soul at his feet as their one only lover. Of these latter Shree Radha was the chief. This Radha is Shree Krishna's *Para-Prakriti*, is that very self-differentiated Being in and through whom the Lord enjoys and realises His Infinite Love. And here in Shree Brindabana, in the love and life of Radha and Krishna, the eternal relations and reciprocities of Infinite Love were re-acted, so to say, upon a noble earthly stage. Not the upholding of righteousness nor the overthrow of injustice; neither the destruction of evil-doers nor the protection of the virtuous;—none of these were the objects of this Brindabana-*Leela*. The lofty spiritual plane where this love-play was acted, —and where, indeed, it is being eternally acted—is beyond both Good and Evil. It is the plane of Pure Love, The object of this Leela or Sport, and indeed of the very advent of Shree Krishna in Brindabana, was mere sport. It was pure enjoyment. This *Leela* or *Avatara* was an end unto itself; or if any end can at all be ascribed to the Sport of the Lord, that end was His own Love. For His Own Love's sake, Shree Krishna manifested this Brindabana-*Leela*.

And the Bengal school of Vaishnavism holds that the object of the *avatara* or descent of Shree Chaitanya Mahaprabhu was nothing less than the fulfilment of this Supreme Love of Shree Radha and Shree Krishna. There had been, they say, an eternal yearning of Shree Krishna to taste the love that Shree Radha always bears for Him. He is the object of that love; even as Radha is the object of His love. This love is eternally drawing them to each other; Shree Radha is continually losing Herself in Shree Krishna. Shree Krishna too is continually losing Himself in Shree Radha. Yet they never really know the other's love as it is in itself. This is the supreme sweetness and, at the same time, the eternal tragedy of all love. We want to see it from the inside, we want to taste our lover's love, as it affects and is tasted by him or her. We feel we are very sweet to those who love us; and we yearn to taste that sweetness ourselves. We know not how sweet, how lovely, how beautiful we are; our lovers alone know it. And as we see the glow of this love and bliss in their face, we yearn to feel ourselves how it really is. This is love's highest bliss and deepest pain. And even as we yearn to know, feel, and taste directly, and in the fullest measure, that wonderful love which flows out of our lover's hearts and makes them forget themselves, even so Shree Krishna yearns to taste and feel the love with which Shree Radha loves Him. This is really the supreme secret of the Radha-Krishna *Leela*. This is at once the highest happiness and the saddest tragedy of that love. Shree Radha's love is absolutely pure. There is neither sense nor self in this divine passion. Shree Radha looks at Shree Krishna, and her form fills out with fresh beauty and fresh sweetness, from moment to moment. She looks at Shree Krishna and drinks in His Beauty, and at every sip grows in superb beauty herself. And this beauty draws Shree Krishna to Her. And as Shree Krishna approaches Shree Radha, Her beauty grows step by step and more and more. It grows endlessly and eternally. And it growingly and eternally increases the passion of the Lord. It grows until the love of Shree Radha seems almost to absolutely beggar the Lord of the Universe. He whose name quenches the thirst of all creatures, burns with this unquenchable thirst of the love of Shree Radha. He who fills the infinite worlds, cannot fill the heart of Shree Radha. The more He gives the more she yearns to have Him more and more. And even Shree Krishna knows not and cannot solve this mystery of the Love of Shree Radha. For how can the *Purusha* know the love with which His own *Prakriti* loves Him ? How can mere man-love sound the unfathomable depths of true woman-love ? The *Purusha* must Himself be His Own *Prakriti*,—the man must first be a woman, true and loving,—before he can truly know what the love of *prakriti* or of the woman really is. To taste, to know, to feel the supreme love that Shree Radha gives Him, Shree Krishna had, therefore, to become Shree Radha Herself. And this was the object of Shree Chaitanya *Avatara* or the descent or incarnation of the Lord as Shree Chaitanya Mahaprabhu. In and as Shree Chaitanya, Shree Krishna took unto Himself the form of Shree Radha, the *Purusha* assumed the garb and the spirit of His Own *Prakriti*; and He did so only to taste what that love really is, with which Shree Radha, His Own Supreme *Prakriti*, has loved Him from eternity to eternity.

श्रीराधायाः प्रणयमहिमा कीदृशोवानयैवा
स्वाद्यो येनाद्भुतमधुरिमा कीदृशो वा मदीयः ।
सौख्यञ्चास्यामदनुभवतः कीदृशं वेति लोभा
तद्भावाढ्यः समजनि शचिगर्भसिन्धौ हरीन्दुः ॥

There are three main objects (मूल प्रयोजन) of the Chaitanya *Avatara*, say the Bengal Vaishnavas. And in this text these three-fold objects are enumerated. The first is—what is the excellence and superiority of the love of Shree Radha? Second—what is that Beauty and Loveliness of mine, whose wonderful sweetness is tasted by Shree Radha with this love of Hers? And third—what is the nature and measure of the enjoyment and happiness that Shree Radha gets from my love? Yearning to know and taste these, Shree Krishna came and was born in the womb of Shree Sachi Debi, the mother of Shree Chaitanya.

This was the inner necessity of the advent of Shree Chaitanya. All the previous incarnations, with the exception of the Brindabana-*Leela*, were moved by what might be said an outer motive. Pity was the force that impelled the Supreme Being to incarnate Himself in the previous ages. The necessity was man's and the creation's, not really and directly of the Lord and Creator Himself. But Love was the motive-force of His incarnation in *Dvaparh-Yuga*, when He came down in His own true and proper form and in all His fullness, and sported at Brindabana with His own *Prakriti*-s or His own differentiated selves. The Gopinees or the cowherds of Shree Brindabana were His own limbs and members, so to say; they were parts of His own Being, and instruments and vehicles of His emotions, His *rasa*-s. As the Son is the very being of the being of the Father, eternally joined to, yet eternally differentiated from the Father in Christian thought and speculations, even so not only Shree Radha, but all the lads and lasses as well as all the elders of Shree Brindabana are the very being of the being of Shree Bhagavan or the Supreme Person, eternally joined to yet eternally differentiated from Him. Shree Krisnna is Bhagavan. Shree Krishna is the Perfected Form of all Emotions and all Bliss. He is *Nikhila-rasamrita-murti*. But the emotions need vehicles and instruments for their fulfilment. And the infinite emotions of Bhagavan demand adequate vehicles and instruments for their self-fulfilment. These emotions are many; but some are ephemeral and some are permanent. The permanent emotions are four—(1) *daspa* or the emotion of love and devotion of the valet towards his master; (2) *sakhya* or the emotion of love and devotion of the friend towards his friend; (3) *batsalya* or the emotion of love and devotion of the parents towards their child; and (4) *madhurya* or the emotion of love and devotion of the lover towards his or her object of love. Shree Bhagavan is the source and satisfaction, both the norm and the form, of all the emotions. Whatever is not *in* Him cannot possibly be in this world. All these relations of love have their perfect form and fulfilment in the Being of the Lord. This is why these are spiritual relations and not merely a movement of our carnal affections that are to-day and cease to be to-morrow. And to realise Himself as *Nikhila-rasamrita-murti*, the Absolute separates Himself from Himself, and by this eternal act of self-differentiation, creates within His own Being these vehicles and instruments of His *rasa*. This, in brief, is the philosophy of what the Vaishnavas call Brindabada-*Leela*, or the Sport of Shree Krishna in Shree Brindabana. But in this Brindabana-*Leela*, something was left unfulfilled. Shree Krishna, who excels in evey quality, could not excel Shree Radha in the quality of Her Love, She left Him a debtor. It was to discharge that debt, to feel the supreme Love of Shree Radha in His own self, that Shree Krishna assumed the form and spirit of Shree Radha in Shree Chaitanya Mahaprabhu. That was the inner need of the Chaitanya *Avatara*.

But as in every incarnation, so here in the incarnation of Shree Krishna as Shree Chaitanya Mahaprabhu, there was an outer object also. But this object too was somewhat different from that of the previous incarnations. This outer object was allied to the inner object. This object was to reveal to the world that supreme ideal of piety which the world had never known before. The older Dispensations had promulgated new social orders and had introduced new rituals and sacrifices into the world. Salvation before was either through knowledge or gnosis, as in the Upanishads, or through *yajna*-s or sacrifices as in the Brahmanas of the Vedas. But all these were either too difficult or too abstruse or had fallen into disuse in this present Kali-*Yuga*. If salvation could not be attained except either through gnosis or *Jnanam* or sacrifices or *karma* then no one could possibly attain it in this age. Salvation had to be made easier of pursuit and attainment for the weaker and degenerate race of modern mankind. And this was the outer object of the incarnation of Shree Chaitanya Mahaprabhu. This easy way was the way of *bhakti* or Love. *Bhakti* means the worship of the Lord through the emotions. And the first step towards the cultivation of this *bhakti* was chanting the name of the Lord. To preach the name of Shree Krishna, to induce people to repeat His name with love and humility, and thus to train them for the enjoyment of the sweetness of that pure and bright *bhakti* which the world had never known before, was the principal outer object of Shree Chaitanya's *Avatara* or descent or incarnation.